ON COMPETITION
IN ECONOMIC THEORY

By the same Author

Published by Macmillan

MANUFACTURING BUSINESS

FAIR TRADE (with Frank A. Friday)

Published elsewhere

OXFORD STUDIES IN THE PRICE MECHANISM
(Contributor and Joint Editor)

CAPITAL DEVELOPMENT IN STEEL

THE LIFE OF LORD NUFFIELD
(both with Elizabeth Brunner)

ON COMPETITION
IN
ECONOMIC THEORY

BY

P. W. S. ANDREWS

Official Fellow of Nuffield College, Oxford

MACMILLAN

London · Melbourne · Toronto

ST MARTIN'S PRESS

New York

1966

MACMILLAN AND COMPANY LIMITED
Little Essex Street London WC 2
also Bombay Calcutta Madras Melbourne

THE MACMILLAN COMPANY OF CANADA LIMITED
70 Bond Street Toronto 2

ST MARTIN'S PRESS INC
175 Fifth Avenue New York NY 10010

PRINTED IN GREAT BRITAIN

THIS BOOK
IS DEDICATED TO MY PARENTS
AND ALL WHO HAVE NOURISHED
AND SUSTAINED ME OR THE
THEORETICAL TRADITION
WHOSE HERITAGE
I SHARE

When the Stranger says: 'What is the meaning of this
    city?
Do you huddle close together because you love each
    other?'
What will you answer?

T. S. ELIOT
from *Choruses from 'The Rock'*
in *Collected Poems 1909–1935*
(Faber and Faber, 1936)

CONTENTS

vii

PART II
A CRITIQUE

A. Application to Non-retailer Firms

B. Application to Retailer Firms

NOTE TO THE SECOND IMPRESSION

I HAVE not wanted to do more than make small verbal clarifications and corrections of misprints, which a reissue can carry. (These occur on pp. ix, 5, 7, 32, 41, 49, 65, 75, 80, 87, 111, 112, 124, 126, 128, 130, 132, 138.) I have been warmed by the reception of this work in letters from colleagues in divers parts of the world, and this note gives me the chance to make two comments to which some have urged me and which further readers may find useful. First, this is a short book but it covers a lot of ground and probably has to be read as a whole, if the force of the argument on any one theme is to be appreciated. One important example: the section concerning retail trade theory should perhaps not be read in isolation by those with specialist interest; nor should it be skipped by the general theorist. The separate attention to this subject is because the paucity of orthodox work specifically directed to this area made it necessary for me to present positive analysis of my own, in order to come to grips with issues which simple extensions of orthodox theory purport to cover; but the whole discussion reflects back to the major themes of the book. Second, apart from that section, this work concentrates so much on criticism because, at this stage, it has seemed to me desirable to force concentration on the general defects which there are in the prevalent methodology. Criticism, if valid, requires no further justification, but I am in any case entitled to plead that I have elsewhere published, and worked with, an alternative theoretical system, which is free from the criticisms here brought against orthodox static marginalist equilibrium analysis. The basic text is *Manufacturing Business*, first edition 1949, special consideration of capital investment theory being contained in *Capital Development in Steel*, 1951, written jointly with Elizabeth Brunner. (Those interested in a simplified pedagogic model of the price theory may be referred to an article by Miss Brunner which will appear in the *Revue d'Économie Politique*.)

Oxford, July 1966   P. W. S. A.

BY WAY OF INTRODUCTION

> . . . I do not agree that discussions about method
> are 'time wasted in quarrelling' . . . . There has
> for some years been too much abstention from it
> among economists. . . —J. H. CLAPHAM, 1922

THIS book criticizes the static marginalist equilibrium method
of analysis of the individual firm, and has still broader implications. Although the analysis is critical in form, I write out
of a belief in the high importance of economic theory and in
the positive worth of evaluative stocktaking for the further
development of economics. It may be of interest, therefore,
to review the background from which the book has been
written, by way of an introduction to it.

The analytical method which is under criticism played, in
fact, a part of the greatest importance in the creation of that
vision of the interconnexions of economic society which is
the hall-mark of the trained economist. Developments in the
application of that method during the last generation or so,
however, have produced hesitations, and in some ways a con-
flict of vision, at the most general level of economic thinking
for the very reason that these developments have been concerned with the unit of activity which lies at the heart of
economic theory—the individual firm, as economic theory
conceives it.

The static marginalist equilibrium method is 'marginalist'
in so far as it turns on the relationships between the marginal
revenue and cost functions which are conceived to be considered by the entrepreneur as he decides price, output,
capital investment, or any other quantity of economic interest.
It is in terms of these marginal functions that the entrepreneur is considered to maximize his net revenue, or 'profit'
(so that 'profit maximization' has no general definition and
has to be interpreted in the terms of whatever analysis is

I

being used). His optimum choice is that which would leave him with no marginal incentive to vary it for so long as the conditions external to the firm, but affecting the positions of the marginal functions, remain unchanged.

Within the terms of this micro-equilibrium system, whatever the particular form of marginal theory which is applied, the internal economy of the firm as a whole may be seen as a system of functional relationships which are consistent with each other because of the common elements of the techniques applied within the firm and the market circumstances in which it is assumed to be set, and also because of the common net-revenue-maximizing objective of the choices which the entrepreneur is assumed to make.

If a firm is assumed to be in a perfectly competitive situation, with regard both to the sale of its products and to the hiring of factors of production, the whole micro-level analysis becomes greatly simplified—e.g., market price is the marginal revenue from sales/output and at any level of market price the individual firm has an infinitely elastic demand, so that output is to be decided solely with regard to the variation in costs; similarly, the market price of any factor of production is the marginal cost of obtaining it, and the employment of a factor is effectively determined by its marginal productivity at that price, marginal productivity itself being resolvable into the marginal physical product determined by technical factors, and the market price of that product. It will therefore be readily appreciated that, through the simple analytical connexions with the markets in which it operates, the internal analysis of the firm meshes in with the analysis of economic society as a whole.

The classic vision of the economist is, therefore, that which was nurtured in the application of the static marginalist method in the theory of perfect competition. The analytical vision then runs continuously from society as a whole, through industries, and down to the activities of individual firms. In this perfect integration of the pricing system (taking for granted of course the full employment of the economy), the valuations of final output by the ultimate consumer can be seen as determining, given the state of technology, the values set upon factors of production as a consequence of the bidding for factors by entrepreneurs influenced by productivities, so that consumer valuations will be 'reflected upwards' in the individual costs which determine, against the valuations placed by consumers on the goods to which they relate, the extent to which the production of any one good is justified as against that of other goods which may be produced from the same scarce resources.

As economists moved over, from general social analysis and the broadest generalizations about the movements of prices of important commodity groups, to closer attention to actual problems of industries and firms (as was increasingly the case during the first thirty years of this century), it was found, however, that this perfect competition framework as fully developed had two defects from the point of view of its realistic applicability. First, for the equilibrium method of analysis to be applied in terms of perfect competition, marginal costs of production had ultimately to rise, and must not remain unchanged or fall, with increased output. It was therefore *prima facie* inapplicable to many actual cases. Second, the theory seemed rather tenuous, in so far as the perfect competition firm lacked body; in a perfect market, with standard goods, the choices facing the individual firm are so straightforward that the term 'decision' is too strong. It has, for one thing, no selling problem and the analysis has no room for selling costs of the kind of advertising whereby firms may be thought to help to determine the kind of market conditions which they face.

The upshot of consideration of this problem was the development of theories which started at the level of the firm, in which it faced a market where it had some choice over price, and which it could apparently manipulate by expenditure on selling costs. These newer theories of imperfect and monopolistic competition belong to, and generated others of, the applications of the static marginalist equilibrium method which are considered in this book and we shall not go into further details of them here.

4 ON COMPETITION IN ECONOMIC THEORY

The general point which arises is that these newer theories kept to the marginal methodology. It is true that monopolistic competition theory recognized the possibility of oligopolistic situations and, there, the orthodox analytical method continued to yield indeterminate analyses. But the impact of this was delayed because attention was concentrated on the determinate analyses. The result was the development of a kind of double vision, but it was one with which the economist could continue to live without methodological disturbance.

At the one level, perfect competition theory could be kept in all its details with a clear conscience, as a theory of perfection which could be used for the assessment of the condition of any situation which would be consonant with maximum economic 'welfare', and for the corresponding criticism of any divergent conditions in the actual world. More reluctantly, it was also kept for the general economic analysis of economic society and of the effect of broad social forces, simply because it was very difficult to get a generalized view on the basis of the newer quasi-monopolistic theories which were applicable to firms.

At the same time and at the other level, the newer theories themselves were a powerful attraction towards further work, since at last we had some theory which looked like coming to grips with reality. The newer theories, moreover, assumed special importance since they seemed to point directly to important policy conclusions regarding the economic functioning of business.

There were strains, as may be imagined (and recalled) from this duality of analytical vision, but with the interest of the Keynesian discoveries at the social economic level and the new areas for work opened up in industrial economics, practising economists had a good deal of excitement in prospect. The strains of teaching a duality of theory were partly relieved by the fact that at each level the same determinate marginalist method could be employed; the very excitements of all the newer development in theory also helped; pupils do not raise methodological worries when tutors can point to new conclusions which seem worth the training costs.

What happened next, of course, was that economists found that they had to worry about oligopoly. Curiously enough, it was the invasion of one level of analysis in the interest of the other that provided one of the occasions for the emergence of a greater degree of methodological discomfort. I am referring to the Oxford researches, in which I was more or less accidentally involved, where business men were asked about pricing in the interest of the implementation of Keynesian policies. Since then, with interruptions due to the 1939–45 war, there has grown up a much more general awareness of the practical importance which oligopoly situations are likely to have. This is the consequence of work by many economists, both of an empirical and of a theoretical kind.

The formal results of this in terms of the application of static marginalist equilibrium method may be studied in the first part of this book. To summarize the upshot as I see it, the vision of economists is in danger of becoming confused, following some confusion of theoretical reactions. So far as general theory and teaching are concerned, the predominant effect has been to strive to keep the marginalist methodology, despite the fact that it is indeterminate in the face of oligopoly. On the one hand, oligopoly is denied as having practical importance or, in other 'revisions' of theory, it is simply ignored, so that determinate analyses of the monopolistic kind may still be used. On the other hand, oligopoly is recognized but there is an appeal to the probability of collusion between businesses and collusive situations may be analysed in terms of monopoly, and so yield determinate results. There is, however, yet another type of reaction, which is to throw over the methodology, and economic theory with it, and appeal to behavioural factors and other non-economic entities.

With it all, there has developed a much greater strain both in being an orthodox economist and in teaching orthodox theory. Those of sophisticated temperament may carry on in an eclectic fashion, but increasingly there may here be discerned some tendency toward cynicism as to the value of economic theory itself, once one gets away from the large truths of economics. Such people are naturally drawn to practical problems which can be handled more as matters of administration than as involving economic subtlety, and it may well be that from this angle will come new progress in detailed theory applicable to their problems.

But there is not much help here for the large number of economists who are trying to carry the Keynesian analysis forward in the study of problems such as the economic growth of underdeveloped areas. As I have already indicated, they are faced with large problems of 'disaggregation' which cry out for relevant and related theories at the level of the industry and the firm.

Nor can these take comfort from economists who are specializing in researches at the level of actual industries nor from the majority of trained economists actually engaged in the business field. Even casual contacts here will surely suffice to reveal a considerable degree of cynicism with the relevance of the orthodox training at the micro-economic level.

Of course, all this cannot continue for ever. Some time economics will have to take a good hard look at its methodology and where it has been getting. It seems clear that this appraisal will have to start at the level of the firm, where our present discomforts began. But it will not rest there. No matter how useful as a basis for broad generalizations we may decide that the classical theory of perfect competition may be, we need to make a much more complex and detailed use of it than its methodology will permit. We need to build a general theoretical system which will be consistent with a view of the micro-economic phenomena with which we can be happier than we can with orthodox theory. It is in the belief that the time is right for this process of reappraisal to start now that I have published the present book.

———

The criticisms of the marginalist equilibrium methodology which I offer in this book were originally formulated by me in the course of studies of individual businesses and of industrial groupings and they played their part in the development of my own theories in the area of the firm and of the industry.

It may be of interest that my industrial researches were originally designed in the light of the body of theory which I now criticize; it was only as one circumstance or another led to objections to details of the method which I was trying to apply that I found myself necessarily thinking in different terms, as I was gradually forced to construct a theory which would be a useable, and a testable, guide in further investigation of business circumstances and policies.

The first (confidential) report on the research into Courtaulds alone, for example, was forced into a monopolistic small-group mould, with some revision of my views about cost functions, but otherwise with Courtaulds as a simple market leader. Going on to Courtaulds' competitors led to a drastic revision of this one-firm view of the market and to the beginning of a realization of the competitive impact of industrial structure. But rayon was an oligopoly explicitly, and some revision of orthodox theory here was not, in retrospect, surprising since that theory itself did not yield a single-form solution. The researches into businesses making boots and shoes to which my colleague, Elizabeth Brunner, and I next turned were taken up precisely because we thought they would provide 'illustrations' of the practical application of monopolistic (large-group) theory. The consequence, after attempts to get what we found re-cast into this mould, was the realization that oligopoly was a much more widespread phenomenon, and further studies of individual businesses in other industries led to the first generalization of my theory.

In 1949 I published a theory for business in the manufacturing sector which differed in kind from orthodox theory and in which the analysis of price for the individual firm was linked on to the Keynesian approach to the general economic activity, besides integrating generalizations for the product market with circumstances in the factor markets in a way consonant with local oligopsony and Keynesian interdependence.

I have already indicated one answer to the natural question why I did not publish any detailed criticism of orthodox theories as soon as I had evolved it. I was myself trained during the period of the emergence of the newer theories of

B

the firm and was conscious of the importance of the work which the pioneers involved had done; my own work had been done under their shadow as it were, and I preferred to write as positively and directly as possible but in a form so that, for example, the differences between my theory and that of monopolistic competition should emerge quite clearly in the course of exposition.

If I did not publish such a critique I was, of course, led to adumbrate it in academic discussion. Soon after the publication of *Manufacturing Business*, I was induced to enter into critical appraisal of orthodox theory, first in graduate theory seminars at Oxford and then in a long *viva voce* dispute with the late Professor Koopmans of Rotterdam in the course of a visit to the Netherlands arranged by Professor Meij, as well as in more formal expositions at the Netherlands School of Economics and at the University of Groningen.

In 1958, on the suggestion of Professor Austin Robinson, I gave a paper on modern theoretical approaches to industrial competition to a conference in the oil industry and the critical details which I necessarily covered there have attracted useful comment and encouragement from others. I was prevented from following this up, had I been so inclined, by heavy work involving economic evidence in the Restrictive Practices Court, which, itself, made the publication of a general critique of orthodox theory seem more desirable, for I had begun to see how theoretical concepts hindered the orthodox approach to practical industrial situations.

In 1963 Miss Brunner and I visited the University of Pittsburgh and the lively discussions of theory in the Faculty Seminar which we organized in the Graduate School of Business there, and which were associated with interviews of business men by the seminar, also forced further realization of the potential productivity of critical work. Preparation for the Bley Stein lecture at the University of California, Los Angeles, towards the end of our visit reinforced this. On return to England I was therefore pleased to have an invitation to lecture and hold discussions in the Faculty of Law of the University of Paris in terms which required me to lay a foundation of criticism of orthodox theories. This latter visit was saddened by the death of Professor Robert Goetz, so that my main lecture became a memorial tribute and our hopes for research and other collaboration in the future were frustrated.

For the purpose of my Paris visit, however, I had prepared some material and I made some limited circulation of this together with the English text of my lecture, mainly to those associated with the Oxford Economics of Industries seminar. I had representations that I should publish this material, especially from the senior colleagues associated with me in this seminar. In the event, it seemed to me desirable that I should now publish a rather more full account of my critical views, and this book is the result.

Personal acknowledgements. What started 'by way of introduction' has necessarily taken on some of the characteristics of a Preface and involved me in that expression of a sense of obligation to others which I should like to continue in this present place and not to transfer to a more orthodox position in the book. I have already referred to stimuli before the actual writing of this book in its present form. Lady Hall and Mr. D. K. Stout are warmly thanked by me in this connexion. Looking back from the present over the past, I think I should mention the continuous stimulation and encouragement which I have received from members of the Oxford graduate seminar in Economics of Industries. I hope that Professor Morris Adelman of the Massachusetts Institute of Technology who tried to get me to do something like this a while ago is not disappointed. I am sorry that I could not submit my text to my old friend the late Professor Robert Goetz. Sheer obstacles of space and time prevented me from using this book as a basis for continued discussion with Professor Neil Jacoby of the University of California, Los Angeles. I have, however, enjoyed continual discussion and critical encouragement from Elizabeth Brunner and Professor Bela Gold, currently working with us on leave from the University of Pittsburgh. Professor Gold has been a source of warmth as well

as light when I have been struggling with difficulties of con-
cise exposition. I should like to end, however, with special
thanks to Elizabeth Brunner, who has been my colleague in
practically all the studies of businesses which have underlain
my theoretical work, and with whom, of course, I have had
many discussions of the economic theory of our field of study.
I know that she will not, yet I hope that she will, regard this
book as in some sense her product as well as mine. My sense
of obligation to all those whom I have thanked by name, and
indeed to the various institutions—to which I should add the
Warden and Fellows of Nuffield College, my academic home
since the first piece of Courtauld research and before—requires me to say that, where so many have the right to my
gratitude, no-one is to be burdened with responsibility for
any defects or shortcomings in the final product.

Turning to the pleasant task of thanking those who have
been closest to me in the making of the book, although for
the first time I have not been able to call on my family as
proof-readers, I thank my wife for the constructive tolerance
which she showed while I was writing. My secretary, Miss
Carol Kovach, typed the many drafts of the ms. with cheer-
fulness and accuracy on top of a heavy load of other work.
I have received very practical encouragement and support
from my publishers and from Messrs. R. & R. Clark Ltd.,
the printers. Finally, I wish to thank Mr. T. S. Eliot, O.M.,
and his publishers for allowing me to use the quotation from
Choruses from 'The Rock'.

PART I
A REVIEW OF MODERN THEORY

PART I

A REVIEW OF MODERN THEORY

---

1. INTRODUCTION: MICRO-EQUILIBRIUM THEORY

This part of the book puts forward what I regard as substantial criticism of the general theory of the firm as it has developed since the death of Alfred Marshall. We are therefore concerned with the economic theory which uses the concept of the equilibrium of the individual enterprise in the analysis of competitive industries. The reader is asked for the moment to hold back any query which may have arisen from my using the word 'competitive' without any qualifying adjective, for more will be said about this.

Reference will be made to individual authors who have made distinctive contributions, but we shall not embark on any detailed comparison of even a sample of the textbooks using this methodology, which is so widely taught and used that it may seem to have become part of the universal methodology of economics. By way of general reference, the kinds of original sources which I have in mind are (in the order of our later reference):

E. H. Chamberlin, *The Theory of Monopolistic Competition* (Harvard University Press, 1st edn. 1933; 6th edn. 1950)

Joan Robinson, *Economics of Imperfect Competition* (Macmillan, 1933)

H. Hotelling, 'Stability in Competition', *Economic Journal*, 1929

A. Smithies: *inter alia*, 'A Theory of Value applied to Retail Selling', *Review of Economic Studies*, 1939, and 'Optimum Location in Spatial Competition', *Journal of Political Economy*, 1941

W. A. Lewis, 'Competition in Retail Trade', chapter v in *Overhead Costs* (George Allen & Unwin, 1949)

J. R. (now Sir John) Hicks, 'The Process of Imperfect Competition', *Oxford Economic Papers*, February 1954

13

W. Fellner, *Competition among the Few* (New York: Alfred Knopf, 1949)

W. J. Baumol, *Business Behaviour, Value and Growth* (New York: The Macmillan Co., 1959)

R. F. (now Sir Roy) Harrod, *Economic Essays*, Part II (Macmillan, 1952)

J. S. Bain, *Barriers to New Competition* (Harvard University Press, 1956)

The general works of Samuelson carry over the resulting system of doctrine into authoritative general analysis, but he is one of the most austere of mentors. Almost any recent general textbook, and perhaps managerial economics textbooks especially, will be found not only to be designed to inculcate this system as the central core of economics itself, but also to illustrate the contortions which result from the attempts to handle 'practical' matters which such texts are bound to make.

There is a history to this methodology lying back in the development of the 'general equilibrium' and of the 'Austrian' schools of economics, but we shall not be concerned with this.[1] As I have indicated, it was after the death of Alfred Marshall that this system irrupted into what may be thought to be the mainstream of English and American thinking. It may now be seen to have frustrated, and not to have furthered, the development of the Marshallian kind of analysis.

Marshall's own methodology avoided commitment to assumptions of equilibrium at the level of the individual firm, through his use of the 'representative firm' as his unit of micro-analysis.[2] That device is itself open to objections with which we shall not now be concerned. It is, however, to be

[1] To one brought up eclectically in Continental and Marshallian systems of thought, as the present author was, it has always seemed that here lay one of the main reasons for that lack of sympathy with Marshallian analysis which Schumpeter had, although he recognized the greatness of Marshall as an economist—cf. his *History of Economic Analysis* (New York: Oxford University Press, 1954) especially chapter 5, section 2.

[2] Ref. Andrews: 'Industrial Analysis in Economics—with especial reference to Marshallian doctrine', in *Oxford Studies in the Price Mechanism*, ed. Wilson and Andrews (Clarendon Press, Oxford, 1951).

noted that the Mathematical Appendix, Note XIV *bis*, and other parts of his *Principles of Economics* indicate that Marshall was aware of the considerations which were to lead others to take the plunge into modern atomistic equilibrium theory.

What Marshall and the later economic theorists have very much in common is a broad view of the real world to which their analyses are to be applied. I therefore pause to say something about the kind of real world (perhaps better put, the sector of the real world) to which modern micro-equilibrium theory may be thought to be applicable. It would be as sterile to ignore this context of application as it would be to neglect the historical context within which our modern scientific ideas have developed. Since economic theories are not intellectual or aesthetic toys, indeed, it is not surprising that there should be some relationship between these two contexts, and we shall in fact look at each in turn.

2. THE CONCEPT OF OPEN COMPETITION

Thinking about the business world with which modern micro-equilibrium theory is concerned in its discussion of outputs, prices, capital investment, and so on, I select the phrase 'open competition' to characterize what seems to me to be its essential feature. I choose 'open competition' because, whilst it refers to competition as a phenomenon, it has not so far been used by others and so has not any special theoretical implication. Indeed, except in so far as the word 'competition' itself has 'value' overtones (and even these have been sharply changeable from generation to generation) it is also mercifully free so far from either approbatory or damnatory implications.

More specifically, modern theory has developed with reference to manufacturing and distributing industries. Agricultural and extractive industries were not seen as presenting the theoretical difficulties which engendered the modern system of analysis. Indeed, these areas do not seem to have

had fresh general theoretical attention for more than a generation. We shall therefore formally confine ourselves to the
manufacturing and distributing industries which are relevant
to the historical context of the theories we shall be discussing.[1]

The *essential* characteristic of an industry which is in open
competition, as I define it, is nothing more than that such
an industry is formally *open to the entry of new competition*.

The question of number of firms. Of course, we all know that
it is traditional to restrict the application of any 'competitive'
theory to industries where a number of businesses are more
or less directly in competition with each other. We shall have
to come back to this question and it will follow from my later
argument that an industry with only one firm in it might well
have to be analysed as though it were competitive. For the
present, let us leave the question of number on one side but
recognize that all that my definition does is to exclude cases
where the entry of new competitors is not possible, or where
there are more or less permanent restraints on the number of
competing businesses. If we adopted any more restrictive
definition of open competition than the one that I have proposed, we should find ourselves compelled to treat the theories I am going to criticize as though they fell into several
distinct classes. It seems far more correct to see them as one
body of theory which grew quite naturally out of, by contrast
to, the classical theory of pure competition—or, rather, the
theory of pure competition which evolved from the classical
approach to competition.

3. THE REAL CONTEXT OF CLASSICAL THEORY

Most of the industries with which classical economists
were concerned had a sufficient number of businesses for
them not to think, down to the time of Marshall, of applying

[1] However, my general methodological criticism of micro-equilibrium
theory must also have application in any realistic consideration of these
primary industries, for there, too, it would seem difficult to justify handling the changing position of individual businesses in a changing world in
terms of their necessarily being at rest.

the theory of oligopoly, or certainly not that of duopoly, which is where the problem of oligopoly was usually left—hence the traditional reference to number at which we have already glanced. Further, such industries showed prices which were usually compatible with one another, in the sense that commodities with similar specifications generally sold at much the same prices; and also that prices of commodities with different specifications could often be analysed as compatible with each other on a cost basis. Moreover, these, provided that there were sufficient steadiness in their national environment, normally showed a short-run steadiness of prices. (I refrain from calling this an equilibrium state and, if forced to give it a name, I should prefer to borrow, I hope fairly, the term 'steady state' from the physical sciences.) Any notable changes in commodity prices could frequently be referred to changes in cost conditions, and short-term breakdowns from any such 'steady-state' of prices would ordinarily be associable with abnormal changes in the balance between capacity and demand.

Supply and demand theory and the emergence of the theory of the firm. Classical theory used the assumptions about number of businesses to justify a condition that individual businesses in any industry should accept the market price as they found it, and adjust their supply to it, even though movements in aggregate supplies would affect market prices. Theorizing in terms of single-product industries, this theory could therefore proceed in terms of the balance between the demand at any price and the supply which would be forthcoming at that price.

Such a supply and demand analysis would, perhaps, be found by anyone not trained in it surprisingly adequate for the problems to which the older economists confined themselves. The applications of classical theory, indeed, make it understandable that not much attention was paid to the question of the equilibrium of the individual business. The individual business, in fact, was but a term in the industrial analysis. It was, however, quite well-known, as a matter of practical fact, that, if an industry achieved a sustained expansion of output, costs of production averaged over output might well not rise, and might indeed fall, in the long run.

Supply and demand analysis allowed for this, as we know, by incorporating supply curves which remained constant or fell, as well as those which rose. In all this, what was the position of the individual business? To us, who are the children of the history of thought in this area, it may seem both inevitable and right that the equilibrium of an industry *should* be taken to entail the equilibrium of its individual firms. Marshall, who was certainly not less a mathematician than those who boldly insisted on this, would appear to have been unhappy that he could not go so far as them with 'the mathematical method' but, nevertheless, as we have noted, his own methodology stopped short of this. I am myself now prepared to assert that such a micro-equilibrium is not essential to the general methodology, but that is to be one of the upshots of this book.

Marshall, with his mind on the 'ordinary business' of life, was no systematizer for the sake of a system. The implications of the definition of a perfect market (as much accepted by Marshall as by any), when explored by puristic mathematical theorists, made it necessary to argue in terms of the equilibrium of the individual business. Requiring the full, short-, or long-run, atomistic equilibrium of the industry, their methodology made explicit the necessity for the equality of marginal cost and marginal revenue.[1]

With this development, the 'theory of the firm' took its place alongside the 'theory of the industry'. The history of professional thought since then would appear to be that of a war between the two which ended in apparent victory for the theory of the firm and twilight for that of the industry—a theme which we shall come back to later on. Meanwhile, I merely note that the twilight of the theory of the industry has

---

[1] The fact that 'marginal revenue' was not christened until later does not affect the validity of this generalization, for this was but a renaming (by Mrs. Robinson) of the derivative of revenue necessarily used in the mathematical exposition of profit maximization (cf. Harrod 'Notes on Supply', *Economic Journal*, 1930, where he uses 'the increment of aggregate demand curve').

had important effects for the handling of short-run effects of economic conditions. For one thing, industrial structure ceased to have any part in the discussion even of cyclical conditions. In the greater part of our own discussion, however, we shall confine ourselves to longer-run conditions and to the historical context within which the modern theory of the firm has developed.

The equilibrium of the individual firm. It was, we may recall, with regard to long-run supply conditions that there originated the discontents with classical theory which Clapham[1] hinted at and Sraffa[2] brought so clearly to light. Only increasing costs with increasing output at the level of the individual firm were compatible with its maintaining its equilibrium within a competitive industry, for its marginal revenue was necessarily analysed as constant at the level of market price, so that it might dispose of any output it could produce at no significant reduction of price.

As already noted, it was known that conditions were otherwise in some manufacturing industries which were

[1] Ref. J. H. Clapham, 'Of Empty Economic Boxes', *Economic Journal*, 1922. See also Clapham, 'The Economic Boxes: a Rejoinder' [to Pigou], *Economic Journal*, 1922: 'Finally, I do not agree that discussions about method are "time wasted in quarrelling!"' . . . 'There has for some years been too much abstention from it among economists, due in part to a certain very natural piety. Things are constantly said in conversation which never get into print, and we need, as one of us would say, to bring inside and outside opinion into line.'

[2] P. Sraffa, 'The Laws of Returns under Competitive Conditions', *Economic Journal*, 1926. 'The striking feature of the present position of economic science is the almost unanimous agreement at which economists have arrived regarding the theory of competitive value, which is inspired by the fundamental symmetry existing between the forces of demand and those of supply, and is based upon the assumption that the essential causes determining the price of particular commodities may be simplified and grouped together so as to be represented by a pair of intersecting curves of collective demand and supply.' . . . 'And so, with the lapse of time, the qualifications, the restrictions and the exceptions have piled up, and have eaten up, if not all, certainly the greater part of the theory [represented by the supply curve].' . . . 'The really serious difficulties make their appearance when it is considered to what extent the supply curves based on the laws of returns satisfy the conditions necessary to enable them to be employed in the study of the equilibrium value of single commodities produced under competitive conditions.' . . . 'It is necessary, therefore, to abandon the path of free competition and turn in the opposite direction, namely, towards monopoly.'

ordinarily discussed as though competitive analysis were applicable. Contact with industrialists brought a general awareness that there were widespread expectations that rising outputs would bring reductions in costs. The accepted economic theory now made it necessary to interpret this in terms of a stability of autonomous individual supply.

Within the micro-equilibrium methodology, there were only two ways in which such a stable situation could arise: The first alternative (1) was that marginal revenue should fall, with increasing output, faster than marginal costs fell; the second (2) was that some form of costs, which were not included in those costs ordinarily brought into the analysis and which could be shown to be relevant, should rise sufficiently sharply so as more than to counterbalance any fall in 'costs of production', as ordinarily considered. It is relevant with reference to later theory that it had become usual to ignore costs of transport and marketing and any other 'selling costs' when discussing the equilibrium of price.

4. INTERPOSED CRITICISM OF HOTELLING-LIKE MODELS

To avoid unnecessary complication of the subsequent exposition it appears possible to dispose of one theoretical development which seized on the second alternative listed in the preceding paragraph. This type of construction originated with Hotelling, and in its subsequent application, e.g., in the works previously cited by Smithies and Lewis, it has normally had reference to retail industries.

In view of the stress on irrationality in the theories which took the other alternative route, it is noteworthy that this type of construction assumes that consumers are rational in their preferences and choices. It is therefore assumed that prices *at point of consumption* must be identical in equilibrium conditions. In the type-models, consumers are, however, rigidly located along a road and are therefore variously separated from producers. Attention may therefore be concentrated on delivery costs. To secure expanding output, the individual producer must reach more distant consumers; according to the way one looks at it, 'non-production' costs rise, or 'net receipts' fall, at the margin, and so, even in a competitive market, these may counterbalance any falls in production costs proper.

Subsequent discussion will show that I myself find it attractive to assume that consumers are generally *not* irrational. But the kind of theory we are now discussing has fatal defects for any applicability to a world in which consumers ordinarily move about during, as Marshall would say, the ordinary business of life. Even an economist who does not, as I do, boggle at assuming irrationality, must, I suggest, be very wary of a theory which assumes as an alternative that consumers are, in effect, paralysed.

This consideration seems so overriding that I do not pursue other matters, especially because we should then be concerned with features which this class of theory has, in any case, in common with the theoretical models we must discuss otherwise—e.g. the single-product firms and the closed or severely restricted entry of new competitors to the industry concerned. In principle, in terms of methodology, the Hotelling-like models, it will be seen, belong to the class which we are now considering.

5. THE ALTERNATIVE METHODOLOGY: THE RECOURSE TO INDIVIDUAL DEMAND CURVES

The introduction of the concept of the individual demand curve for the firm marks off the theoretical methodology which has dominated modern economics. In this way, the theoretical dilemma described on page 20 was resolved in the first of the alternative directions which we then distinguished. Falling demand curves entail falling marginal revenue curves and these can counterbalance falling costs. The vital question, however, is—what is the economic basis by which one can get such conveniently falling marginal functions?

How, precisely, are the falling demand curves to be understood?

The methodology of Joan Robinson. Seen from this methodological point of view, Joan Robinson's demand functions have no analytical roots. Her demand curves fall simply because she tells them to do so. By this device she virtually assumed that the major theoretical problem had been solved, without actually solving it. It may well be argued that such 'implicit theorizing'[1] is and must always be illegitimate, no matter how many times theoretical economists may have resorted to it. There was certainly no analytical basis for the policy implications which this gifted author derived from the assumed-to-be-facts both of falling demand curves and of the nice manipulation of outputs by business in the face of a knowledge of such curves.

Some may, however, counter with some such argument as that a theory is to be justified by its results; the apparent stability of outputs in the real world justified an equilibrium approach in theory; the fact of falling cost curves in a number of industries meant that it was necessary to *invent* falling demand curves, if the equilibrium approach was to be used. We shall be entitled to reply to that, that the necessity of *an* equilibrium approach does not mean that it is necessary to assume the *full* equilibrium of the firm, without further demonstration—which would fly in the face of reality—that businesses individually actually were in this happy state, when they exhibited what we are pleased to recognize as stability.

There is, however, yet another objection to this particular kind of analysis and one which may be thought to be deadly: As Mrs. Robinson herself recognized when she wrote the *Economics of Imperfect Competition*, oligopoly, the state where relatively few businesses are in close competition with one another, is very much a problem with which the theory of the firm has to grapple. She admitted that, in assuming that businesses knew their demand curves and that the latter were

[1] Ref. W. Leontief, 'Implicit Theorizing: a Methodological Criticism of the Neo-Cambridge School', *Quarterly Journal of Economics*, 1937.

of a generally-falling kind, she was brushing the oligopoly problem on one side. In consequence she failed to produce a system of *general* analysis and, viewing her work as generating a system which at best could have only particular applicability, it would have been useful had she gone on to explain in analytical terms just when and how her constructions might safely be used. As it was, her final chapter on 'a world of monopolies' suggests a degree of generality of application of her theory which she was not entitled to assert, even implicitly, by the sweep of her generalizations.[1]

To categorize this work as a dead-end may seem an act of base ingratitude to what has been for so long the leading British textbook, and to which, apart from our fundamental criticism, generations of undergraduates have no doubt been grateful for its lessons in the application of geometry to marginal analysis, as well as, more positively, for her 'open-ended' discussion of cost-curve possibilities (which certainly did nothing to close minds, rather the reverse, in this important area). But we have to maintain our central purpose fairly severely in this chapter, and it may at least be said that Mrs. Robinson herself now seems to recognize the essential sterility of this so-much-reprinted text.[2]

---

[1] In the light of this, and of her subsequent theories of other sectors of economics, it is strange to see Mrs. Robinson reproaching later writers for asserting a generality for their theory, without any analytical examination of the basis on which they might claim such a generality, and without reference to their texts to ascertain precisely what kind of generality— much more explicitly open to detailed analytical emendation than her theory was constructed to be—these authors would claim. Ref. '"Imperfect Competition" Revisited' in Mrs. Robinson's *Collected Economic Papers*, vol. 2 (Basil Blackwell, Oxford, 1960), p. 234: 'A debate which consists in defending or attacking "principles", such as the "full-cost principle", "the marginal principle" or the "normal-cost principle", and trying to fit all types of situation into one system is obviously foredoomed to futility.' Similarly, in ' "Imperfect Competition" To-day' in the same volume, pp. 242-3, Mrs. Robinson criticizes the 'line of attack . . . developed under the banner of the "full-cost principle" ' and concludes: 'It leaves us in a state of perfect nescientness—anything may happen. The moral seems to be that the approach to price theory through individual decisions will never lead to fruitful generalizations. . . .'

[2] Ref. *Collected Economic Papers* (Basil Blackwell, Oxford, 1951), Introduction, pp. vii-viii: 'At this point, it seems to me now that I took the wrong turning. . . . Instead of abandoning the static analysis and trying to come to terms with Marshall's theory of development, I followed

C

The Chamberlin models. Superficially, judged only by what develops after the basic assumptions have been taken, there are considerable resemblances between Mrs. Robinson's methodology and that of Edward Chamberlin, so far as the 'large-group' case of the latter is concerned, anyway. Chamberlin's method was more general, however, precisely because it embraced the small group or oligopoly case. It is probable that it is the fact that it had a more extended analytical basis which accounts for the fact that Chamberlin's work has been much more seminal. At the time of its publication it was quickly recognized as a strikingly complete answer to the theoretical problems of the earlier controversy on the theory of costs and prices. Nevertheless, as its author has now explained, this work did not spring out of that controversy but from preoccupations with railway rates.[1]

The Chamberlinian methodology lies at the heart of practically all subsequent theory, and (if only from reactions to this or that detail of it) has played a large part in other ways in deciding the direction in which theorists have felt that they have had to proceed. It is therefore inevitable that what I have to say about modern micro-equilibrium theory should eventually add up to severe criticism of the Chamberlin model, just as a methodological examination of that model is an essential preliminary to the understanding of 'mainstream economics' after it. Another occasion and a purely historical context would be required for proper discussion of the historical importance of Chamberlin's book, and for a proper appreciation of the level of completeness which it attained despite the novelty of its thought.

Pigou and worked out the *Economics of Imperfect Competition* on static assumptions.' See also Mrs. Robinson's verbal quip, reported in *Monopoly and Competition and their Regulation*, papers and proceedings of a Conference held by the International Economic Association, edited by E. H. Chamberlin (Macmillan, 1954), p. 507: 'Again, as on the day before, Mrs. Robinson made a plea for replacing the static equilibrium theory by a dynamic approach more relevant to modern conditions. "I make no apology for having written my book twenty years ago," she said, "but I find it shocking that people still read it."'

[1] Ref. E. H. Chamberlin 'The Origin and Early Development of Monopolistic Competition Theory', *Quarterly Journal of Economics*, November, 1961.

In every science, there seems to be a time when older methods of thought are so ingrained that they dominate a work even of a revolutionary kind, so that, in the end, it is found to suffer from similar inherent methodological defects. Nevertheless, the truly seminal work prepares the ground for a real advance just because it makes it easier for subsequent theorists to get at what had hitherto been mere inchoate error. To a theorist in our present field, I suggest that Chamberlin's first edition will remain a classic and a beautiful book.

Chamberlin's methodology: the 'large-group' model. We may recall that Chamberlin's 'large-group' analysis produced a model of an industry, (1) which was open to the free entry of competitors; (2) where the number of competitors was formally large enough to meet the requirements of pure competition models; (3) where the competing producers sold technically identical products at identical prices; and (4) nevertheless operated with costs which decreased with increasing output in equilibrium conditions; and (5) where firms of equal efficiency, etc., would earn only normal, competitive, long-run profits. It thus seemed to embody the main features of ordinary competitive industries, the recognition of which, so far as characteristics nos. 1-3, and 5, were concerned, had produced the classical theory of competition (see sub-section 3 above), as well as No. 4, whose recognition had produced the methodological crisis we have referred to.

Chamberlin's *falling demand curves* gave falling marginal revenue curves, and so conformed with the first of the two logically possible ways of resolving the decreasing-costs conundrum (see page 20 above). Chamberlin explains such demand curves in terms of underlying '*consumers*'' *preferences* for the products of individual producers, so that, in any given position of prices, it would require further reduction of prices for his competitors to wean 'consumers' away from any particular business; and if such a producer should raise his price, he would nevertheless retain the custom of some of his purchasers.

Chamberlin's analysis also allowed for the effect of *selling costs*, the costs of overcoming existing preferences at any given level of prices and attracting further customers to one particular producer. We should note the historical importance of this concept—for, for the first time, it apparently became possible to discuss the phenomenon of advertising within the system of marginal analysis. We shall later consider some criticisms of this approach to advertising; nevertheless, let it be said that, given the previous feeling that advertising was outside the system of economic analysis, even an illusion of an ability to handle it was far better than nothing. It was a prerequisite of further work; so long as advertising fell outside the scheme of things, it could be tackled only unanalytically. It will have become clear, however, that Chamberlin's handling of selling costs is intimately connected with his concept of buyers' preferences—they are the costs of weaning consumers from present allegiances. They will, therefore, be affected adversely by any fundamental criticism of the assumptions about preferences, and we need not pay special attention to them now.[1]

Although a general criticism of the preference concept is deferred, we should nevertheless establish a criticism of the analysis in which it appeared. Chamberlin's general analysis, of course, made allowance for the possibility that preferences might be unequally distributed—e.g. that an individual producer might have a larger share of the market than a competitor because, at any level of prices, more buyers preferred to deal with him; and that his buyers might have stronger preferences for his product than those of his rival might have for the latter's product, so that the former's demand curve would be less elastic. His simple version of his large-group

---

[1] In later editions of *The Theory of Monopolistic Competition* there are indications that Chamberlin might find acceptable an alternative treatment of selling costs, on the analogous basis of delivery costs. This, as in the Hotelling model which was discussed on pp. 8-9, might be free from the general assumption of irrational preferences, and, indeed, might generate demand curves net of selling costs which resembled those derived from the preference analysis. The point to be emphasized here is that, in this case, the whole analysis would be vulnerable to the criticism which we have already made of Hotelling-like models so it affords no secure alternative basis for Chamberlin's constructions.

model, however, was formally constructed on the assumption of an equal distribution of preferences—part of the way in which he could put the individual producers in the identical situations which would cause his model to reproduce the parity/compatibility of prices discernible in the real world.

It is possible that this large-group model did not receive sufficient critical attention just because of its realistic reference. Seen from our distance in time, nevertheless, it may be thought surprising that it can have been so readily accepted that the ordinary industries to which it seemed applicable (because of the compatibility of prices to which a single-product model necessarily approximated with an equality of prices) should (even when allowance is made for this abstract simplification) have the distribution of preferences which the model requires if equality of prices is to ensue.

Diversity of size being admitted, the distribution of preferences must be such as to give not only parallel inequality of market shares but also elasticities of individual demand curves which would adequately offset the effects of the diversity of cost positions which would result from mere diversity of size, let alone differences in 'efficiencies'. Yet, once economists got around to discussing preferences in a realistic fashion (usually in 'asides' from the main exposition of the simple models), they soon wrote as though preferences were by no means likely to be distributed in this fashion (e.g. the larger firms were easily thought of as having not only larger shares of the market but also less elastic demand curves). But if one admits non-proportionate distribution of preferences, non-compatible (in the simple model, unequal) prices, rather than compatible (equal) prices, would seem to be the likely result. Such a confrontation with reality should, then, have caused doubt concerning the analysis of preferences, quite apart from the theoretical criticism of the concept of preference in itself, which we are deferring.

The 'small-group' model. Chamberlin's preference concept was also applied in his theory of the 'small group'. This refers to industries where numbers of firms are assumed to be so small that the price-output policy of any one would have not-negligible effects on the situation of others, so that there is oligopolist interdependence between businesses. Changes in the prices of any one producer would have repercussions on the market situation of rival producers so that these latter would readjust their own price-output decisions, and any individual producer needs to make assumptions about such reactions when deciding his own policy.

The case of *closed entry* (membership of the industry being limited to the small number of producers assumed to be there at the start of the analysis) is the only one which Chamberlin has worked out in detail. His solutions are those which are already to be found in classical discussions of the oligopoly problem. The alternatives are: (1) in independent price competition, the prices of all firms will be driven down so that only long-run average costs will be covered; (2) if, to take the other extreme, all producers fully recognize their interdependence, then a monopoly price would be established for the group; (3) if, however, each simply took the other's supplies as he found them, and adjusted his own so as to maximize his immediate profitability, prices would settle at some point intermediate between the extremes of the first two alternatives, the precise level depending upon the number of firms. We should recall, of course, the ingenious use of demand curves in which a more elastic demand curve, which shows the results for sales of independent pricing by the individual producer, *given* the prices of the others, slides up and down a less elastic curve which marks off the business's sales (crudely but operationally put—its 'share of the market'), when it and all other competitors change their prices together, and so do not disturb their individual markets by relative changes in their prices.

Some special criticism of the 'small-group' case. We may pause to notice certain points of criticism which, because of their special applicability to Chamberlin, should not be deferred until our general critique. The first concerns the likelihood that individual producers might know their demand curves so that they could consider the elasticities of these in their pricing policies. In the case of the large group, Chamberlin's assumptions may make it seem reasonable that individuals might have an adequate knowledge of their demand curves, even if only by trial and error, for the distribution of preferences taken together with the large number of competitors would bring a sort of isolation of the individual markets. No-one seems to have considered the peculiar difficulties in the way of such knowledge on the part of small-group producers in the case of the 'monopoly' solution—No. 2 above. If we are to suppose that the knowledge is to be gained by sustained collective experiment, would it not be necessary that the industry be subject to formal cartel organization, not mere tacit, loose collusion?—and it would have to be an unusually lucky and clever cartel at that. On the other hand, any independent trials would bring the alternative solutions— Nos. 1 and 3—as between which the theory is irresolute. It is of special interest that *later* theorists seem to come back to the collusive solution and, of course, this criticism of Chamberlin's model is relevant to them and must be borne in mind when we discuss them.

We may also note that the price-competition solution—No. 1 above—in fact gives too high a level to the lower limit of price when it settles for that price which will yield long-run normal, competitive profits, as the average-cost levels imply. Important consequences follow once this is subjected to criticism. Surely, firms would not give up production as soon as prices fell to long-run average costs? In terms of orthodox theory, which divides costs so that overhead costs are treated as being capital costs (see p. 66, n. 2 below), firms would give up production only when prices fell below short-run average prime costs. All firms, obviously, could not stay at that low level for long, but we must not jump to any conclusion that the process will end in the establishment of long-run-average-cost prices; for if some of the firms, in existence when prices were at this low short-run level, went out of production, those left would still, on Chamberlin's assumptions about the case which we are discussing, force down prices to that same level. Are we to deduce that stable equilibrium can result only if and when the industry has been reduced to but one

firm? Is not, then, the logical result of Chamberlin's case No. 1
that there should be established a monolithic monopoly?[1]

The question of new-entry competition. The monolithic monopoly, which we contemplated in the previous paragraph,
could happen only if new entry competition were barred or
singularly inefficient. I do not follow this 'game' into analysing the fluctuating prices, as between average long-run cost
levels and average prime-cost levels, and the fluctuating
numbers between one and some small number larger than
one which would seem likely to result from admitting free
entry into Chamberlin's case No. 1, according to the general
analysis previously adduced. But this perverse result is a
relatively minor reason why it is strange, in retrospect, that
Chamberlin treated the possibility of new entry and its effects
so shortly as he did.

The formal solution which he proposed for this case was
indeterminate as between the three kinds of outcome which
he had found for prices in a closed group. He treats free entry
as simply reducing actual results, at whatever level of prices,
so that only normal profits would be obtained. This comes
about through the shifting of the demand curves used in his
solutions of his three cases to a tangency position *vis-à-vis* the
cost curves. We have already shown that this simply is not
good enough and cannot be valid for one of his cases, but we
there followed Chamberlin in assuming that in that case new
entrants would adopt exactly the same price policy as the existing producers. Why should they do so? Should not any
such analysis treat new entrants separately and ask how they
are likely to respond to the market situation as they find it?
Is it not plain unreasonable to leave the collusive solution,
No. 2, as Chamberlin finds it?

More, however, will be said about new entry (and the
effect of associated ideas about economies of scale) later in
this part. But in leaving this subject temporarily, we may note

[1] It will be realized that the logic of this part of my criticism appears
to destroy the possibility which Chamberlin entertains, for a very small
number of producers, of fluctuations in prices between the competitive
and monopolistic norms, if businesses behave in such a way as to force
prices down to the former.

that new entry needs reconsideration even in the large-group model. How would an industry in Chamberlin equilibrium, assuming that excess capacity was as serious as the textbook curves would suggest, look to potential new entrants? Surely, we should assume that they have reasonable information about the cost curves. If so, why should they not think, when they look at the high prices prevailing, that the existing firms must be very inefficient and calculate what they would have, at normal near-full capacity, to play with by way of reductions in price and in expenditure upon selling costs, according to Chamberlin's ideas of them, in order to establish themselves in the industry? This is admittedly a 'realistic' criticism, but so long as criticism respects the theoretical structure which it is considering, there seems no reason to exclude common-sense considerations.

The question of oligopoly. Until Chamberlin, oligopoly had been considered rather as a theoretical puzzle than as a situation of any practical significance. Leaving on one side the difficulties which we have raised concerning two of his solutions and the possible effects of new entry on all three, the question remains why he and those who so quickly adopted his system of analysis should have been content with its inconclusiveness as between three modes of business behaviour and policy. The answer would seem to be that professional attention found several reasons for concentrating on the large group case (and, to some extent, it got distracted by the controversy over the differences between monopolistic and imperfect competition, the reasons for which were not immediately apparent in this case).

First, as we have already noted, the large-group model brought into the analysis of industry the features of the everyday world about which economists had been most concerned —e.g., notably, falling costs at the level of the individual firm. Second, within this determinate framework there was the intellectual excitement of being apparently able for the first time to get down to the question of advertising and similar selling costs. Third, Chamberlin at least made it possible for oligopoly to be discussed within the same general system of analysis and the resolution of his inconclusiveness could apparently be left for practical realization when and if actual oligopolies should be under consideration. Another contributing factor was that Chamberlin met with very little fundamental criticism. Macgregor nursed his dissatisfaction until he felt able to present it systematically in 1949.[1] Hicks, who was potentially the most important English critic because of his continued interest in methodological questions, seems to have been too immersed in working with the theory of perfect competition, which was the only framework in which he could tackle systematically the general theoretical problems which interested him. In his famous review of the Chamberlinian development, he cast doubts on the importance of its differentiation of individual products and clearly did not feel called on to pause over oligopoly independently, although that was in itself a consideration which would be bound to be nugatory for the system of analysis to which Hicks himself has been so committed.[2]

So far as Chamberlin himself was concerned, the fact remains that he considered oligopoly to be more important in practice than it had generally been considered to be. He would himself appear to have been bemused by the very determinateness and elegance of his large-group analysis. When, much later, he has been concerned to suggest that other theories, as for example those of myself, really fall within his analysis, he has appeared to overlook that his analysis as such stopped with the large group. Other work may cover similar

[1] D. H. Macgregor, *Economic Thought and Policy* (Home University Library, Oxford, 1949), chapter 2, 'The Representation of Supply'. It is perhaps the curious decision to put it in the H.U.L. which accounts for the sad neglect of this work of Macgregor's old age. Perhaps it might be added that it bears on many other important problems besides that of price.

[2] Ref. J. R. Hicks, 'Annual Survey of Economic Theory: The Theory of Monopoly', *Econometrica*, 1935. Hicks's interest in continuing to use perfect competition theory may perhaps have prevented him from seeing the methodological implications of the development of imperfect and monopolistic competition, or even of his own reactions in favour of the competitive variability of commodities as distinct from their fixed differentiation, in this essay. Although rejecting the implications of imperfect competition analysis he seems to have continued wedded to the techniques of full micro-equilibrium analysis which it generated.

phenomena—such as differentiated products—but it is tack-
ling an area which he necessarily left inconclusive analytically.
Chamberlin has, of course, more recently thrown his large-
group analysis aside. He has done this partly as a result of
Triffin's criticism of him, in which a Walrasian interdependence of the demand for commodities is allowed to swallow up
the industry approach on which Chamberlin depends. But a
major reason has been an increased conviction that oligopolistic conditions are common in industry, and this is a conviction which many economists now share.

6. THE OXFORD ECONOMISTS' RESEARCH GROUP

INQUIRY

It is relevant at this point to consider the inquiry of the
pre-war Oxford Economists' Research Group, whose findings
in the matter of prices were reported in the widely-discussed
article by Hall and Hitch.[1] This latter has played an important part in the wider acceptance of the practical relevance
of oligopolistic conditions and not-always-careful discussion
of it has greatly influenced subsequent theoretical developments.

In brief, the Hall and Hitch article reported that business
men generally settled their prices by procedures which were
based on their average costs, determining in various ways a
pricing margin to be added to their current average prime
costs.[2] Prices in practice tended to be stable because there
were strong penalties for changing them. These penalties

---

[1] R. L. (now Sir Robert) Hall and C. J. Hitch, 'Price Theory and
Business Behaviour', *Oxford Economic Papers*, No. 2, 1939.
[2] It will be seen that my phraseology is devised to cover procedures
which started from any ingredient of prime costs, such as labour costs,
as well as from average works costs or, indeed, average total costs. In my
view no general analytical importance is to be attached to the fact of so
various a pricing procedure, since I see analytical significance only in
prime costs and in the price which is the end product of the 'costing',
and prefer to formulate the matter so that there is no encouragement to
the kind of 'full-cost' mis-reading of Hall and Hitch which I criticize
later.

arose because of the prevalence of oligopolistic conditions—
if any producer should cut prices, his competitors would retaliate and so the demand for his product would be inelastic
in its response to his lower price; equally, if he should raise
his price, he would fear that others would not follow, his
competitors preferring to enjoy the stronger demand which
his higher price would give them, so that he would then suffer
an elastic reduction in demand.

Contrary to what is often asserted, Hall and Hitch put forward no full cost *theory*. In view of the widespread references
to such a theory, it is worth remarking that there can seldom
have been so remarkable a case of the invention of a doctrine,
literally without any text of origin, in order to subject it to
critical attack. We shall not pause longer over this, except to
notice that the point of the attack has been that, presuming
that *someone* believes that business men settle their prices so as
to secure their full costs plus a predetermined profit margin
which would be satisfactory to them, such a procedure must
be irrational in that there can easily be seen to be situations
in which business men would make more profits by doing
something else—a conclusion which allows the critic to go on
advocating an economic theory which in his eyes has at least
the virtue of presuming that the business man is interested in
profits—the majority case; or which allows him to write off
everyday private enterprise business as irrationally conducted
—a procedure no less satisfying to a minority of economic
theorists.

Underlying all this has probably been a confusion of the
statement by Hall and Hitch of an average-cost 'costings'
basis of prices with their recording of business men's beliefs
that *normally* price should cover the full average cost with
fair net profit for a reasonably efficient firm. The belief that
it was fair to approach prices in this way, the principle on
which business men appeared to act when they could consider a price independently, was stated by Hall and Hitch as
the full cost *principle*. But this did not give a *theory* of prices,
and some readers of the article have evidently overlooked the
cases to which the authors drew attention, where business

men stated that they were not able to get the prices which
they would expect on a full-cost basis, whilst nevertheless
continuing to set prices on the average-cost basis which has
been explained.

The paper was also famous for its introduction of the arrest-
ing kinked demand curve, which may perhaps be seen as a
development from the double oligopoly demand curves of
Chamberlin, which Sweezy also made around this time. This
gave a discontinuity in marginal revenue curves at the prevailing price because of the differing elasticities which would
attend a rise or a fall in the price of one product considered
by itself. With the help of this device, marginalist theory
could explain why businesses should adhere to whatever
level of prices existed. But, as Fellner also has noted, this
gave no theoretical explanation of the *level* of price. Even if
the dénouement of the kinked demand curve was consistent
with all that had been taught before, marginal analysis itself
explaining why it could go no further, it was none the less
a rather flat ending to any ordinary course on price theory
to demonstrate to pupils who had mastered the sophisticated
difficulties of marginal analysis that pricing in practice was
not inconsistent with their training. But, of course, matters
have not been left there and economists have continued to
worry about the determination of the level of prices.

Anti-theoretical reactions. We need not pause overlong to
deal with one reaction, which has been to preserve marginal
equilibrium theory as a 'welfare' tool[1]—a rod with which to
beat the practices of the actual world on account of its shortcomings from the nirvana of perfect competition. The theoretical world of welfare theory imports special assumptions
(e.g. with reference to costs, not to mention all the assumptions about income effects) besides that of competitiveness,
and it may be that a suitably amended price theory could
cause an upheaval in that body of welfare analysis which
tends to be taken as settled for all time.

It may, however, be useful to look back at one reaction to

[1] See, for instance, P. J. D. Wiles, *Price, Cost and Output* (Basil Blackwell, Oxford, 1961), chapter 1, especially pp. 3-4.

this theoretical problem because it is fundamentally anti-theoretical in its nature; certainly, when its implications are grasped, it will be seen to be anti-*economic* theory. If business men behave so, and if we cannot find from within our system of analysis an explanation of their conduct, then, it is suggested, they do not pursue maximum profit. (I stress again that the possibility that our existing method of theorizing may give wrong clues as to how profits may be maximized is not considered by those who urge such conclusions.) Adequate profits are a possible goal. Business men want the quiet life.[1] Business life in practice is then a matter for behaviourist hypotheses.

'Snatchers' and new-entry questions. This kind of suggestion may be made by even very distinguished economists. Hicks in his widely-regarded contribution to a symposium following Harrod's reformulation of the latter's own theoretical position,[2] was prepared to see business men as divided, it would appear by temperament, into 'snatchers' who went after very short-run profits, and 'stickers' who were content with a quiet life and planned their investment on the basis of the profits which they thought that long-run competition would leave them.

Without pausing to discuss Hicks's atomistic marginalist model as a whole, it seems relevant to some of our later discussion of new entry questions to note that I find it very difficult to understand his equation of his short-run snatchers with businesses, as he implies, typical of the marginal firms we find coming and going in industries which are in fact easy for new firms to enter.[3]

---

[1] Tibor Barna is perhaps the economist who has most developed this as a basis for a systematic attempt to understand growth phenomena. Ref. *Investment and Growth Policies in British Industrial Firms* (The National Institute of Economic and Social Research, Occasional Papers XX, Cambridge University Press, 1962). See also J. B. Mayers, 'Management and the British Domestic Electric Appliances Industry', *Journal of Industrial Economics*, November 1963; and P. W. S. Andrews and Elizabeth Brunner, 'Business Profits and the Quiet Life', *Journal of Industrial Economics*, November 1962.

[2] Ref. R. F. Harrod, *Economic Essays*, chapter 8; J. R. Hicks, 'The Process of Imperfect Competition', *Oxford Economic Papers*, 1954.

[3] Hicks, *op. cit.* p. 48, 'Marginal firms are thus very likely to be Snatchers'.

In this case, an adherence to Hicks's theoretical instructions for the application of his concept of snatchers in the 'close' period would lead to an idea that such a marginal firm typically expects to make more during the precarious period of its existence than it would expect to make during any later period of survival. The reverse, surely, is the case; relative newcomers among the marginal businesses which may be a feature of some industries surely expect to make less than normal profits during their introductory period. In other words, they will expect relatively great difficulties of survival originally and take the corresponding risk of low profits or losses in the hope that, if they survive to establish themselves in the industry, they will then make substantially higher profits. Incidentally, although authoritative literature has not discussed this point enough, it would surely be a fair reading of it to relate theoretical concepts of 'normal' profits to the profits which are expected *after* successful establishment. (One of the first discussions in the modern context—that of Joan Robinson—would seem consistent with this view.)

All this is consistent with the fact that we may sometimes find new firms which are actually making abnormally high profits. It is probably not misleading to imagine that all new entrants have some idea that they would be, if given the chance, superior in some way or other to the general run of existing firms. It therefore should not be surprising that this should be true of some new businesses during the early period under their founder management (e.g. some of the retailers who have thought up some new way of offering self-service which they think likely to lead to lower costs or to attract more customers to a given site may turn out to have been right). But the very factors which are the foundation of such higher initial-period profits are the things which make successful entry possible (and the parenthetical example of the previous sentence is a reminder that the ideas of new entrants can be both risky and wrong); there is the further relevant point that if a new entrant successfully exploits a new idea it will be copied and exploited by others.

This leads to the further point that Hicks's close period is a very different concept from that of the short run to which he approximates it. (This is quite apart from the fact that since his close period is so tied to the period of setting up the plant it is usually far shorter than a normal period of initial difficulty.) In the short run normal theory takes a business with a given organization and discusses how it, its costs, and so on, will behave if it readjusts its output within this short-period limitation. As we all know, therefore, short-period cost curves take off from any point on the long-run curve. To discuss the experience of the firm during the initial period of establishment of any settled long-run planned capacity takes one into a quite different world.

It is possible to raise an objection to one aspect of these comments: since Hicks's snatchers have their eye on profits during such a short period, it may be said that we should discuss 'normal' profits as though they also were to be defined for such a period. Hicks's snatchers have no long-run life in the ordinary sense, except by chance. Surely this is a quite wrong and misleading use of the idea of normal profits; we need to discuss what economic conditions make it possible for businesses to have this sort of myopia. When we enter the world of shifting and passing demands, thinking, e.g., of those mysterious gentry who seem prepared to run up something as readily for the favours which people will buy on the occasion of a national celebration as for use in national mourning, we remember that preparations for one event may be frustrated by the occurrence of the other. In short, such a kind of 'industry' (defined in terms of suppliers rather than by products) is typically so risky that this class of economic activity might well be discussed explicitly as a kind of gamble.

The introduction of this kind of analytical consideration suggests a warning against introducing such distinctions as that between 'snatchers' and 'stickers' as though such personality differences may be exploited indifferently in the same industry. But such an aberration is only possible because of a fundamental methodological assumption that individual firms, in some sense, have their 'own' demand curves, short-run and long-run, and that they may choose along which curve they will ride. Once again we come back to the influence of atomistic methodology, which it is easy to argue *from* but difficult to argue *to*.[1]

A comment on 'behaviourism'. If Hicks's 'behaviourism' is explicitly introduced into his marginalist framework, we should take note that there are those who start with a presumption that the taking of detailed decisions, within a business, should be studied behaviouristically in terms of decision rules.[2] Here, atomistic methodology has been carried down to intra-entity level and behaviour there is studied without reference to wider context—whether within the firm concerned or within *its* environment. The methodological point of this, paradoxical though it may seem, is that it enables theorists to go on using their equilibrium theory as though Chamberlin's large-group case, or simple monopoly, applied. The individual business man can still be seen as enjoying his 'own' demand curve and choosing whether or not to exploit the position. To the extent to which he behaves like an economic animal, then, orthodox theory can explain the position. If he does not, it can draw, as it seems, important social conclusions from his defect. We shall return to analyses which explicitly rest on this monopoly dénouement later on. So far as the behaviouristic outcome of the manifestations which have just been alluded to is concerned, it seems to me that we should not despair until we have thoroughly re-examined the whole basis of our thinking. We shall certainly need to do so, if our treatment of the real world which we are supposed to analyse is to be more than a series of *id est* propositions.

The attack on Hall and Hitch by Machlup. Whatever may

---

[1] Cf. Macgregor, *op. cit.* p. 35: 'In economics we have to argue *to* diagrams more than *from* them; the diagrams depend on the argument'.

[2] So far as I understand their position, Cyert and March would seem to be imbued with this methodology—ref. *A Behavioral Theory of the Firm: Attempts to Develop a Theory of the Firm which is based on Empirical Studies of Decision-making within the Firm*, by R. M. Cyert and J. G. March (Prentice-Hall, 1963).

D

be the position in more sophisticated texts—and other sub-
sections of this part will show that even acknowledged leaders
of thought in our area are yet confined by similar methodological constraints—there is no denying that the general textbooks have been fairly tough about retaining marginalist-
equilibrium theory and insisting that reality conform in one
way or another, or be adjudged irrational. It would appear
reasonable to suppose that this tendency has been helped
by Machlup's famous onslaught on the Hall and Hitch
article.[1]

We cannot turn aside to develop a full criticism of Machlup's position. It would take some time to follow him through
the ramifications of intertwined argument and suggestion—
and one must recognize that the difficulties of his exposition
were increased by the fact that he was trying to deal with
some other work by Lester at the same time. It does not,
however, seem unfair to put it very shortly that Machlup's
position is that the marginalist theorist need not worry. Since
business men do as they do, *if* they are correctly reported,
one must explain it by profit maximization, and that *of course*
must run in terms of orthodox demand and cost functions.

In the course of his exposition Machlup refers very cogently to the skills which we all, presumably, exercise in the
driving of a motor-car and how we in time come to do it all
unconsciously, as it might be said. This has impressed many
generations of students, but some at least have reflected that
even though they may use their skills unconsciously, they
hopefully drive with awareness of what is going on and of
their own reactions at the time. Indeed one of the ingredients
in the Advanced Motorists test in England is that at any time
the testee shall give a running commentary on the road and
the traffic behind and before him whilst continuing to exercise his driving skills. So that it may be presumed that those
who devised this test have presumed a greater amenability to
conscious description of what one is doing and what one is
reacting to than Machlup would suggest to be normal. Lest

[1] F. Machlup, 'Marginal Analysis and Empirical Research', *American Economic Review*, 1946.

this use of analogy be pressed too far and meet the objection that Machlup was not discussing advanced business men but only ordinary entrepreneurs, let us remark that in a competitive state it is possible to imagine that the most awareful business men might well be deciding the conduct of the others. What is at issue is precisely the kinds of considerations which influence such men. (As to how evidence was got from them, Machlup confuses the Research Group procedure with the ordinary use of simple questionnaires, and Harrod has dealt adequately with this misunderstanding in the Preface to his collected essays.[1])

Even in a brief reference to Machlup, it seems fair to call attention to one passage whose effect would seem to run counter to his main argument. This is the last paragraph on page 543 of his article:

Even without any ethical or unethical code prescribing an average-cost rule of pricing, average cost may be the most important datum for the estimate of demand elasticity. The elasticity of demand for any particular product is determined by the availability of substitutes. In order to estimate how much business a firm may lose if it raises its price, it will consider whether existing or potential competitors can supply competing products at the particular price. The elasticity of supply from competing sources determines the elasticity of demand for the firm's product. The supply from competing sources will depend on their actual or potential cost of production. And usually the best clue that a firm has to the production cost of competitors is its own production cost, corrected for any known differences of conditions.

Machlup leaves the matter there, but there are a number of implications which, to put it mildly, make it surprising that such a passage should appear in the course of an argument explicitly devoted to arguing for a reality, beneath the surface of reported pricing practices, which conforms to some direct sort of confrontation of *independent* demand and supply functions, such as is required by orthodox marginal equilibrium analysis. The puzzle is not lessened by reflecting that Machlup is probably considering longer-run (certainly not

[1] Harrod, *op. cit.* pp. ix–xi.

short-run) situations; for his essay contains no restriction
of his argument to short-run conditions, a restriction which
would anyway be difficult to sustain as being relevant to the
views which he is considering.

The form of expression may be thought to be rather misleading for, by concentrating attention on the *demand* curve
of one firm, it does not attend to the fact that the *supply* curve
of that firm must be presumed to have the same sort of significance for the demand curves of *other* firms. Stripped to the
chassis in this way, Machlup's argument here recognizes a
situation in which an individual firm's demand curve is a very
different entity from the demand curves of orthodox theory.
It does not reflect the basic demand from consumers for its
commodity, but is a statement of the condition on which the
firm will be allowed to enjoy its sales to whatever market it
has—the supply prices of actual *or* (N.B.) potential competitors. Such an equilibrium is not an equilibrium of *output*, in
terms of the counterbalancing of marginal revenue and marginal cost, but is an equilibrium of *price*. Economic theory in
such a case must inquire further, in order to have a basis for
explaining the very thing which Machlup is arguing to be
determinate in a marginalist manner—its output, or output-
scale. Among other things it will have to inquire into the
determination of industrial structure and thus move away
from the individual firm seen as the independent arbiter of
its destiny within the settled market framework given by a
marginal revenue function.

(May I be forgiven for pointing out that the quoted passage
from Machlup may indeed be fitted into my own positive
theoretical framework in *Manufacturing Business* and elsewhere, which has never been offered as an atomistic equilibrium set-up? Moreover, my own theory is explicitly in terms
of an oligopolist situation and, as our discussion of Chamberlin's work shows, orthodox theory has been able to set up
marginalist revenue functions in oligopoly situations only by
giving up formal general analysis and by having uncertain recourse to alternative rigid assumptions about policies adopted
by business men in practice.)

7. METHODOLOGICAL NECESSITIES IN THE ANALYSIS OF OLIGOPOLY

Machlup is so robustly marginalist in intention that he virtually brushes on one side the oligopoly problem which Hall and Hitch raised in so pertinent a form. The first characteristic of the real world which theorists with pretensions to realism have to accept is, it may be repeated, what I have already described as a normal kind of 'steady-state' of prices. When price structures dissolve in a manner which might remind us of the oligopolistic price war of classical kinds of analysis, we can usually find either severe cyclical depression or other reasons for a chronic short-run excess of capacity in relation to markets, and we do not need to explain the resulting price-breakdowns in terms of any *normal* oligopolistic competitiveness. Further, when, more rarely, price structures move upwards away from normal kinds of relationship with costs, we can usually find the basis in chronic and persistent shortages of capacity relatively to demand due to circumstances in which ordinary industrial market forces have been suspended (as in severe inflationary conditions, whether industrial or general); once more we move outside the area of normal theory.

In view of these factors, the determined marginalist theorist has only two alternatives—to deny or to accept the fact of oligopoly. If he accepts the fact of oligopoly, and there has been some considerable movement towards this, then it is difficult to find any refuge in either the precarious equilibrium which Chamberlin thought might prevail with free-price competition, or in the kind of stability of prices which the same author followed classical texts in ascribing to a policy of assuming that its rivals held their outputs constant whilst each individual firm adjusted its supply in order to maximize its gains from the transient situation. In consequence, constructive theory which has persisted in using orthodox analysis has tended to run in terms of some sort of collusion. If he denies the fact of oligopoly, then the marginal

equilibrium theorist tends to be pushed into a kind of construction which parallels that of Joan Robinson in that it is
virtually of a monopoly kind—crediting individual firms with
determinate demand curves of the kind which have their analytical basis in monopolistically separate markets.

8. THE 'COLLUSIVE' SOLUTION OF THE OLIGOPOLY PROBLEM

As has already been said, there seems to have developed
some considerable tendency to favour a solution of the pricing
problem in conditions of oligopoly in terms of some sort of
collusive manipulation of the market by all or a sufficient
proportion of the competitors. Chamberlin himself would
appear now to incline towards this view.[1] The question is,
however, what do we mean by collusion?

No doubt some theorists are prepared to think in terms of
organization of the nominally competing businesses which is
close enough to be tantamount to a cartel. So far as most industries in the U.S.A. or England are concerned, one must
in that case be prepared to adopt the notion of *hidden* cartels.
A recent letter to *The Times* from Kaldor suggests that he
would grasp this nettle boldly.[2] But there are some difficulties
in accepting this view, not all deriving from the illegal status
of such cartels.

Failing such formal cartels, theory must run in terms of
tacit or indirect collusion. The leading specialist text to take
this path is Fellner's *Competition among the Few*, and we shall
consider this as the species-type.

Fellner's solution. Fellner's theory derives directly from
his discussion of the history of oligopoly theory, and this part
of the book in itself makes *Competition among the Few* an
original contribution to economics. Fellner rejects the essentially arbitrary solutions of earlier theorists; oligopolistic interdependence is seen not so much as a hindrance to the orderly

---

[1] 'Monopolistic Competition Revisited', *Economica*, 1951.
[2] Ref. p. 129, n. 1 below.

marketing of products as an opportunity for the exercise of individual initiative on the part of the members of an oligopoly. Fellner's own solution, following this line of thought, is collusive in the sense that, rejecting the complete independence of action which would lead to price warfare or to unprofitable stalemate, he thinks in terms of a quasi-agreement —an acceptance by businesses of modes of behaviour which will lead to a sort of maximization of joint profit.

I say 'a sort of joint maximization' because I shall not go into details concerning the qualifications to the principle, where these departures from his main theme in fact, if analytically pursued, must take us out of the realm of Fellner's principle altogether. The leading examples occur when he discusses such matters as the effects of disparities in individual firms' costs or market positions. But these are embedded in his working out of successive versions of the application of his principle, and the very wide acceptance of Fellner as having found a solution does not derive solely from the fact that his distinctive 'solution' of the oligopoly problem is set in terms which are explicitly consistent with marginalist equilibrium theory. One gets, even after several readings, carried along by, and much of the apparent acceptance of Fellner's concept of leadership as a consistent factor is derived from, his quasi-realistic references to differences in the strengths of firms; e.g., and especially, when he comes to deal with markets which are open to the entry of new competitors, Fellner sees the 'leader' as a large firm, with low costs, high staying power, etc. One tends to miss the point how much he is prepared to depart from his acclaimed principle in such cases. It would seem possible that even he does not see how much he is here discussing the circumstances which may make an equilibrium possible rather than the conditions of equilibrium themselves.

To concentrate more narrowly on Fellner's positive theory, the general idea is that his 'leader' sets a market price for himself, the implications of which, in terms of the positions and shapes of their own demand curves, for their particular markets are accepted by the 'followers' because they do better, or expect that they will do better, by taking decisions which are compatible with it than they would if they took any of the divergent actions which are formally open to them.

The type-model of this situation may be set in terms of Chamberlin's small-group case, with all firms in identical positions. In such a model it is comparatively easy to accept that the leader will maximize profits in terms of the demand curve which each firm will get as its share of the market under such assumed-co-ordinated action. Disparities in market positions, due to product differences and buyers' preferences, and in internal strengths, due to different cost positions, as well as other factors, rule out the general application of such a neat solution (though the idea of it remains fixed in the reader's mind). In such realistically more normal situations, the leader is to be seen, not as the one acting simply for all, but as choosing the price, from the alternatives open to him, which will lead to optimum results *for himself* within the range which will not provoke incompatible reactions from his followers.

Thus, as Fellner complicates his own model, we get rather away from 'one for all' and we are increasingly in the presence of a business which dominates its industry by reason of its strength and does the best it can with that, having regard to the necessity of not driving the followers to set up incompatible break-away movements. For our present purposes, I wish to criticize the ideas about what leadership does, rather than what it is; so I shall not pursue this question very far.

It will be realized that the ultimate strength of a leader depends upon the extent to which he can best stand the losses which he may bring on himself as well as on the other parties if he has to enforce his leadership. Therefore, as has been said, Fellner's leader is generally a low-cost firm. But a strength thus assessed in terms of possible price warfare has importance in other situations only in proportion to the freedom of action which the 'large' firm has then.

It must be noted that initiative, and therefore leadership, in situations actually provoking price warfare is typically exercised by smaller, weaker, but more desperate, firms. In other situations it is difficult not to regard Fellner's leader as rather a sort of *deus ex machina* whose credibility is derived from the fact that it often does appear to be the largest firm which takes the initiative when the level of actual prices is changed. Can that situation not be seen more simply in other terms? Surely, others cannot safely raise their prices if the big firm does not, and practical experience shows that this is quite compatible with pressures (i.e. leadership?) from the others on the big firm to raise its prices when, as in the typical rising-factor-price position, they will all tend to want to do so. (It is not irrelevant, although the fact must not be taken in other contexts, that so many of the inquiries of the Monopolies Commission and of similar bodies have shown that the biggest firm does *not* invariably have the lowest costs.) Similarly, if such a firm lowers prices, the others will have to follow; once again a gloss from experience must add that often this merely regularizes a situation in which quoted prices are tending to get out of line with realities and where the *smallest* firms are already doing more than nibble at prices in their own offers, and so are acting as market leaders.

So far as concerns what the leader *can* do in a Fellner model, the threat of new entry leads to Fellner's strongest qualifications of the joint-maximization-of-profit hypothesis. But the recognition of the entry factor is limited by his seeing newcomers as rather small, open to bullying, and so on; so that the incumbents of an industry have some scope for securing higher-than-entry-attracting prices by joint action or by mutually compatible actions. Further, the force of new entry is rather damped by the general character which is assumed for the markets of individual firms.

Leaving particular points on one side, the fundamental fact remains that Fellner's potential profits are derived from his view of the possibility of the quasi-monopolistic exploitation of market demand curves. In criticizing such a general concept—as we shall have to do in the next Part—we shall also be dealing with the fundamentals of his model. It would throw our discussion out of balance to discuss all Fellner's qualifications concerning his model more thoroughly, but the

48   ON COMPETITION IN ECONOMIC THEORY

fact does seem to be that they eat up his model. And the point remains that, even in situations in which he thinks that monopoly profits would not be attainable, the benefits from his oligopolistic collusion are as monopolistic in kind, from the general theoretical point of view, as are Chamberlin's profits.

Fellner's profits come from monopolistic manipulation of the market via the 'share of the market' demand curves. The other models which we have to consider give up the Chamberlinian distinction between 'share of the market' and 'particular' demand curves, demand functions resolving themselves into single functions which we have already characterized as simply monopolistic. We have criticized Fellner's use of his own kind of demand curves rather than the concept of them. It is the very idea of the 'particular' demand curve which will come up for criticism later. The point remains that, even though Fellner's demand curves are undoubtedly valid short-run concepts, it is not easy to accept that firms could know them at all readily. Precisely the same difficulties of course arise with regard to Chamberlin's share of the market demand curves since the same entities are involved (see page 29). It may be thought that this consideration is in itself an obstacle to Fellner's theory which would have to be overcome before the feasibility of its practical application could be admitted.

9. NON-COLLUSIVE SOLUTIONS

Baumol's Analysis. In *Business Behaviour, Value and Growth*,[1] although explicitly discussing 'oligopolistic firms', Baumol cuts the oligopoly tangle by denying the relevance of

[1] I should note that I am not dealing with Baumol's attempt to construct a theoretical *growth* model for the individual business, for this is outside the context of the static equilibrium theory which we are discussing, which will also be relevant to Baumol's later work. Any detailed criticism of this latter, however, would have to raise serious questions about the economic quantities which determine the firm's apparent choice between profits and sales (ref. p. 1086, *American Economic Review*, December 1962, 'The Theory of Expansion of the Firm', by William J. Baumol). Baumol's article deserves much more careful consideration than

the kind of interdependence between businesses which, from Cournot to Fellner, has been thought to be characteristic of industries where there are few firms, and which, as we have seen, many theorists have come to think to be an important factor in many other industries. ' . . . *in day-to-day decision making*', he says, 'oligopolistic interdependence plays only a small rôle'.[1]

It is possible to have doubts concerning the validity of this judgement. Baumol refers to his consulting experience but the possibility remains that he did not at his level of observation observe a continual glance over the shoulder at competitors' prices and other signs of oligopolistic competition in operation just because pricing *practices*, in routines below or alongside that level, were such as not to invite this kind of conduct in normal times. It is to be hoped that he has maintained continued observation of the developments after some manufacturing businesses have, e.g., taken his advice to raise their prices or to lower them, since he indicates that he has on occasion advised drastic departures from normal policy. We do not, however, need to consider this matter now.[2] The relevant point for the present discussion is that Baumol may, in view of the wide interest in his book, be taken as a leading example of those who, while discussing the general run of industry, reject the collusive solution of oligopoly theory and maintain models in which individual firms face and exploit their 'own' markets.

I have been able to give it, but it seems to me we are there still in an analysis behind which lurk static revenue functions—note the functional form of the choice referred to. We are also still in a world of oligopolies without the characteristic oligopoly problems. It seems to me that any theory of the growth of an individual business must start with a revitalized theory of the industry. Pending further reconsideration, this present essay provides its own note perhaps on Baumol's peroration (page 1087): 'I will only suggest what appears to be the most important point, that our discussion has shown the standard apparatus of marginal analysis and mathematical programming to be fully applicable to decision problems, even when management's objective is not the venerable profit maximization of economic theory'.   [1] *Op. cit.* p. 27; italics in original text.

[2] The sentences following immediately after the sentence cited in the previous paragraph suggest the possibility of important qualifications, and might in themselves raise some doubts about the generality of the application to oligopoly conditions which Baumol claims for his theory.

Generally speaking, Baumol's firm is acting on its own. He differs from ordinary marginal equilibrium theorists so far as the *effect* of his theory goes, quite substantially, in that he does not presuppose any drive for maximum profit. He sees the driving object of a firm as being to maximize its total sales, subject to the requirement that the firm earn a minimum level of profit. Baumol recognizes that there may be an analytical connexion between sales and profits, but he has been struck by the use of sales as a score-board by management and believes that to the business man sales have indeed 'become an end in and of themselves'. His profits constraint recognizes that businesses do not pursue sales without regard to profit.[1]

The *method* of Baumol's theory, however, falls more nearly within an orthodox framework. The market context within which a business is to be thought of as maximizing its sales in a Baumolian sense is represented by orthodox revenue functions for the individual commodities which it produces. For any one product, the possible sales revenue is a function simply of the physical quantity which the business puts on the market, and can be read directly from 'curves of the usual variety' which, Baumol comments, 'require no explanation'.[2] Formally, therefore, a Baumol business may freely choose between lower physical sales at higher prices and higher physical sales at lower prices.

In any *single-product* model (and the question of multi-product models will be discussed later) it will be seen that, since the analysis runs within a given demand curve for the firm, the market situation of a Baumol firm resembles that of a Chamberlin large-group firm, or that of a textbook monopolist for that matter. The theory therefore falls, as I have already indicated, in main principle within the *class* of analysis which I am criticizing. That his firm will not put prices at the same monopolist level as a Chamberlin firm or a collusive oligopolist may be supposed to do does not affect this generalization, even though the real consequences of its behaviour will therefore be very different.

[1] *Op. cit.* chapter 6, esp. pp. 45-50.   [2] *Ibid.* p. 65.

In principle, Baumol asserts merely that a firm is to be seen as imposing a minimum acceptable profit restraint on its maximization of sales policy and he indicates that he would be prepared to accept any broad rule which is consistent with this. The level of such minimum profitability, whatever the rule, is related loosely to such considerations as keeping the shareholders quiet. Thinking along these lines apparently leads Baumol himself to adopt a minimum profits requirement which is related to the total investment in a firm. In any short-run situation this requirement therefore runs in terms of a fixed minimum total of profits, the firm requiring to earn not less than this total.

Referred to a single-product model, then, Baumol's profits constraint is to be seen as adding, to the average cost of any output, a minimum profit requirement which will fall hyperbolically with increases in output. One can then read off the firm's price/output at the intersection of the combined average cost-plus-profit curve and the sales revenue (demand) curve. At that position, the firm will have attained the largest sales which are compatible with its profits requirement. ' . . . the firm always earns only enough to satisfy its profit constraint. . . .'[1]

It may be of interest to notice that the sales maximization objective, which Baumol has indeed some justification for believing is a real objective of business, has to be *written into* his model just because his revenue function is of the 'usual variety'. When some of my criticisms of such a revenue function are taken into account, it is possible to conceive of the sales-maximization objective being *implied by* the form of the revenue function itself. In other words, one can conceive of sales revenue functions being such that to maximize sales is to maximize profit and in respect of which one does not come up against the difficulty which his revenue functions force on Baumol—that maximum sales revenue according to them, without a restriction such as that entailed by his profit constraint, 'might require prices so low that the costs would nowhere be covered'[2]; losses or no, to maximize sales might well

[1] *Ibid.* p. 73.   [2] *Ibid.* p. 49.

be the best that could be done. It is the apparent choice offered by his demand curve that constrains Baumol. This means that the sales-maximization objective could arise directly out of a theoretical model of the market situation of a firm; but in such a case the satisfaction of the firm's objective would be a question of dynamics and would take us out of a static position.

We have concentrated so far on the application of Baumol's profits constraint to a single-product model because of the comparability with the other theories which we have been considering. It is a real merit of Baumol, however, that he does try to cover multi-product firms and, indeed, the details of my single-product application therefore may be somewhat misleading from all but the strict methodological point of view. Baumol stresses that the application of his constraint is to the business as a whole and he handles a multi-product business in a marginalist fashion which could not be applicable in a single-product model.

Within the overall constraint, a multi-product business is conceived of as allocating its resources so that alternative marginal revenues would be equalized. It follows that the single products of such a business would not uniformly earn the profits which the business as a whole would be constrained to make. It is, moreover, this formulation which enables Baumol to preserve the ideal marginalist allocation of business resources as between individual products. The fact remains that the whole construction is dependent on the correctness of Baumol's assumptions about the form of his revenue functions, already indicated as a matter for criticism.

It may be that the allocation analysis is the reason why Baumol found it attractive to retain orthodox monopolistic revenue functions and to apply his profit constraint to the business as a whole. I feel bound to comment, however, that I do not understand this application of the profits constraint, given that Baumol has had such extensive consulting experience. I cannot imagine it being applied as between products with quite different specifications and markets, but in any case Baumol has ruled out some of the very important considerations which then arise, because his monopolistic revenue functions allow no room, for example, for the consideration of the varying competitive position of the firm or of the market situation surrounding any of its products. (This is a quite different point from the fact that, around the average profit imposed by the minimum constraint for the firm as a whole, individual products will show different profit rates. Baumol gets such a result as the more or less automatic consequence of equi-marginal substitution of products—see page 67 of his book. It is relevant to what follows that, as Baumol says, 'This yields no simple pricing rule. . . .')

As a mere realistic comment, at the levels where day-to-day pricing decisions are taken, I am used to seeing products normally dealt with on their own, and have yet to see managers supplied with tables of profits for the whole enterprise, and cannot imagine them doing the calculations product by product which would preserve Baumol's assumed objective. I have already noted a passage where Baumol recognizes the important discussion of competitive responses which can take place in the very kind of pricing decisions which come up for top management to consider.[1] In such cases, of course, his whole method of analysis is inapplicable, and he does not try to cover them.

I should further say that I find it difficult to accept the idea of a minimum aggregate profit constraint for pricing in short-run situations (and Baumol's whole construction is of a short-term kind). Surely, if output dropped off cyclically, with a shift of demand curves to the left, etc., we cannot think it normal that a firm should put up its prices at all, let alone increase them disproportionately to its presumed-to-be-rising average costs? and, if it did so, would it not be less likely to earn as much towards any profit targets?

All this is not to deny the dynamic importance of the top management of a business finding that they cannot earn, or are not earning, what they regard as the minimum reasonable profit for their business in the then-present circumstances; but what they, or shareholders, or take-over bidders, will do

[1] Ref. note 2 on page 49 above.

54   ON COMPETITION IN ECONOMIC THEORY

about it is another matter and takes us right outside the framework of Baumol's analysis.

Harrod's reformulation of imperfect competition. The last major author whom I have selected for consideration is Harrod. The new essay, 'Theory of Imperfect Competition Revised', which accompanied his republication of his earlier articles on the subject in his *Economic Essays*, has the intrinsic importance that it contains the latest thinking of an economist who made significant contributions to the pre-war cost and pricing controversies. (The catharsis achieved by the publication of Chamberlin's and Mrs. Robinson's works frustrated further development of the, in some ways quite distinctive, analytical contribution which Harrod made, e.g. on the operational significance of long and short periods in cost analysis, as well as further attention to some of his questions, e.g. on the significance of ideas of normal profit.) Subsequently Harrod had taken a leading part in the researches of the group from which came the Hall and Hitch article. The publication of the new essay touched off a series of articles in *Oxford Economic Papers*, to which Hicks made the contribution to which we have already referred.

This essay is not easy to discuss. One difficulty of which I am very conscious is that, as Harrod made clear in the private correspondence with me to which he refers in his Preface, he deliberately set out to write what he had to say in terms of corrections to and adjustments of the methodology of the older imperfect competition analysis.[1] Moreover, he felt constrained to keep to the definitions of terms employed in the earlier essays which were to be reprinted as companion-pieces, even though he had certainly become dissatisfied with some of them. (I think that this accounts for some of the difficulty which he would appear to have encountered in the handling both of matters relating to normal profit and some of the conclusions which he had by then come to in the matter of costs.)

Harrod's article as published is, however, all that he has

[1] On all this see, in particular, the first paragraph on p. 140 of *Economic Essays*.

publicly contributed to recent discussion, and we must treat it as it is, allowing that it may well be that it is what he felt to be a dictated form that has forced him so squarely into the class of theory that we are now criticizing. I have, of course, re-read our correspondence, my share of which, as Harrod hints, was fairly lengthy, and, although insistent on some points which I shall now raise again, was undoubtedly not even as clear as I might hope to be on our difficult topics nowadays. I certainly raised the question of his demand functions, which, after all, is the major reason for his coming into the present context. Nevertheless, it may well be that he would have done this in a different way had he not been so anxious that his new wine should not burst old bottles.[1]

In the essay, which we are of course reviewing only in our present context, Harrod retains conventional demand curves but modifies the way in which they are to be understood in order to allow for the effects of new entry competition as he conceives them. Despite his reference (on p. 144) to the possibility of a new entrant being an existing firm, and his recognition of the importance of 'potential competitors' from such firms, he treats new entry as having only quite long-run effects. He explicitly rules out the question of oligopolistic relationship (pp. 151 and 163) even though the new entry postulates must affect this matter too. Whether this be the constraint of an 'old bottle' or not, Harrod is, then, writing consistently within Robinsonian 'imperfect competition' as we have earlier differentiated this from Chamberlinian competition. With that identification, our criticism could, for present purposes, be left, were it not that to go further will

[1] Since this is my first public reference to this correspondence, I am glad to recall how grateful I was, within a short period of Harrod reading *Manufacturing Business*, not only to receive his warm appreciation of what I was trying to do, but also for the generosity with which he allowed me to see him studying courteously, and even accepting, some of my most troublesome ideas. Let me also say that I have had pleasure from my earliest relations with Chamberlin, despite continued disagreement on points which have been important to each of us. He will see that I now acknowledge error in my whilom loose identification of imperfect and monopolistic competition!

E

raise some interesting questions relating to the short-term equilibrium of an industry which have not come up in the longer-run analyses which have been appropriate for other writers.

For the short-run Harrod retains a Robinsonian demand curve which can be as inelastic as one likes for the sake of example; the idea of a varying elasticity would, no doubt, be defended by reference to the varying strengths of buyers' preferences. Viewing this short-run demand curve as the moat around the individual firm's market in the short run, the acceptance of the concept of new entry as considerably easier than older theory had allowed it to be, causes Harrod to think of a long-run demand curve which would be much more elastic. He describes this, rather than forces it into any crucial diagram. That may be the reason why he has not asked himself how he would explain why the competition of new entrants is to be conceived substantially as allowing an individual business, open to such competition, to be able to enjoy significantly higher prices provided that it puts up with substantially reduced sales, as compared with the prices at which it could sell more normal quantities. (This point is legitimate, because even a gently sloping demand curve will allow of relatively substantial increases of prices if the reduction of output is taken far enough.) The fact is that, although Harrod argues *to* his long run all right, he never theorizes *in* it. When one conceives that a new entrant can enforce a lower level of prices generally, why should he not eat into any position, given a still longer run?

Returning to the short run, one's regrets increase that Harrod did not examine again the logic of the descending demand curve which is capable in his view of being markedly inelastic. If new entry can come from existing firms, just how long-run must we conceive that competitive possibility to be? It is clear that Harrod was thinking of businesses going into quite different lines, but even that is consistent with their having a good deal of equipment and know-how, prestige, etc., which they can deploy quickly. I regret that, at the time of our correspondence, I had not so explicitly developed the ideas of 'cross-entry competition'[1] that I was to press later, but they were already factors in my presentation of the argument to him. When one allows for cross-entry possibilities, Harrod has no longer a clear short period before the storm of the long period can hit a short-sighted firm. Even, then, a short period demand curve in the sense of some of his applications, might be so contaminated by the effects of competition, and therefore might so much reflect the cost positions of competitors, that it would cease to be capable of explanation along the lines of buyers' preferences. To have considered such a possibility might have caused Harrod to tarry a little longer with the idea of long-run demand functions which were entirely dependent upon cost conditions, so that, not merely the orthodox theoretical derivation of them, but also the logical reason for their separate existence would have disappeared. But we should then have been facing the question of industrial equilibrium without atomistic equilibrium which I was urging upon Harrod and which, methodologically, his desire to use the old bottles of imperfect competition made him put on one side, when he made the, as he thought, simple reservation that he would not handle oligopoly conditions. In our correspondence I was the whole time asserting the significance of the oligopolistic relationships implicit in Harrod's constructions, but I think I can understand now why Harrod seemed to want to resist just this point. In declining formally to introduce oligopolistic interdependence within his industry he was of course removing the possibility of the most immediate kind of cross-entry competition.

10. A NOTE ON COST FUNCTIONS

It has not been relevant to the main theme of this Part to discuss the treatment of cost functions. However, when we turn to the general criticism of the body of theory which we have been reviewing, we shall find that the behaviour of costs, as a firm varies its output or the scale of its production, can

[1] See p. 78 below.

have a bearing on demand functions themselves. It seems desirable, therefore, to end with a sub-section on the treatment of cost functions in the orthodox theoretical approach to the economics of the firm.

If, in view of Chamberlin's account of the genesis of his theory, it cannot be said that the modern theories of the firm originated entirely in the controversy about costs which was mainly conducted in the *Economic Journal* from 1926 onwards, it certainly seemed, at the time, that the appearance of Joan Robinson's and Chamberlin's books in 1933 terminated that remarkable concentration of theoretical interest. What happened was that the modern theoretical approach to the firm, from its birth, took over the U-shaped cost curves which mathematical theorists had developed in their exposition of the equilibrium of the firm in conditions of perfect competition. The next generations of economists, brought up in the cradle on the diagrams of Chamberlin and Joan Robinson, absorbed such functions *ambulando*.

It is easy now to see that such curves need not have been given this precise form, and doubtless mathematicians originally saw them but as an elegant specific form of the function-type. A downward-sloping branch of any kind would have been adequate to illustrate the dilemma that, if a competitive firm's output or scale should bear such a relationship with cost, then *either* it was not in perfect competition, *or* it could not be in equilibrium *at any time*—and would, in the latter case, be driven to continous expansion, given the infinitely elastic demand which the definition of perfect competition entailed. The precise location and limited range of the lowest reach of the cost curve which a U-shape gave had, however, theoretical attractions because it both generated the welfare implications of that 'optimum scale', which would be enforced by conditions of perfect competition, and showed up starkly the wastes of the departure from this optimum which 'actual' differentiation of the market must entail.[1]

[1] The tendency to conduct simplified analyses in terms of identical firms and the introduction in more sophisticated analyses of the 'rents' of firms with different contemporaneous levels of efficiency or resource

If the development of falling demand and marginal revenue curves marked the first-generation theorizing on the atomistic equilibrium of the firm in conditions of imperfect, or monopolistic (large-group), competition, the fact that the great historical dilemma *had* been resolved on the demand side would appear to have led to a continued demand-fixation of equilibrium economists' attention. More recently, theorists who have been trying to tackle the 'oligopoly problem', under some concensus that this is of practical importance, have continued to try to take their fences on that side of the analysis. As we have seen, the concept of equilibrium, which itself led to the problem, has been kept by the rejection of the analytical significance of the strictly-defined oligopoly conditions themselves—indirectly, by the postulation of collusion; alternatively and directly, by the unanalytical assertion of demand functions which are determinate in spite of those conditions.

Throughout the post-Chamberlin discussion, then, marginalist-equilibrium theorists continued to think from these conventional curves, and an increasing tendency to make 'realistic' asides that cost curves in practice might be more shallow, etc., has not, until Harrod's latest essay, led to any consideration of the effect such qualifications might have on the nature of the equilibrium itself.

Harrod, in his revisionist essay, went so far as to recognize that short-run direct cost curves might be horizontal for considerable stretches of output and that long-run curves might run into stretches of constant costs. (He could not handle within his analysis a falling long-run cost curve.) As we have seen, he attached importance to the possibility that business men might translate easy-entry into long-run demand curves which were relatively elastic. In his diagrams expounding crucial steps in his analysis of price formation and of the determination of output, however, his long-run demand curve does not appear. His refusal to take account of oligopolistic conditions meant that he argued within the limitations of his

also caused this particular formulation of the cost curve of the individual firm, upon which theory concentrated its attention, to be a factor in the disappearance of industrial structure as a subject of theoretical interest.

short-run demand curves rather than attend to the implications of his long-run demand curves. It would seem a reasonable interpretation of his exposition that new entry, following
a 'foolishly' high price, would cause such short-run demand
curves to move to the left, but, because of his adherence to
the archetypical differentiation of an imperfect market, he
could not allow for their elasticity being significantly affected.[1]
He moves from an instantaneous position to the long-run
consequences to demand without, as it were, pausing for
analytical breath.[2]

On the non-independence of cost and demand functions. As
this Part has foreshadowed, it is possible to question the analytical independence of cost and demand functions, which
marginal equilibrium theorists take for granted and which,
indeed, is essential for the formal validity of their work. This
would, I suggest, be a valid point with reference to Harrod's
revision of imperfect competition theory. That it is possible
to make such a point suggests the possibility that economic
methodology may have turned full circle upon itself: The
Economic Journal controversy which preceded the emergence
of modern theory really got going with Sraffa's 1926 article
on the laws of return, and this raised precisely this question
with regard to the industrial supply and demand curves of the
older competitive theory. That this question did not trouble
Sraffa about his own proposals at the level of the firm was,
no doubt, precisely because his sketch of the possible resolution of the decreasing costs dilemma invoked the inviolate
demand curves of theoretical monopoly which were to become an obstinate element in the English traditions from Joan

[1] See the diagram on p. 180 of Harrod's essay and the accompanying
remarks.
[2] Cf. H. R. Edwards's interpretation of this aspect of my new-entry
theory on p. 43 of Competition and Monopoly in the British Soap Industry
(Clarendon Press, Oxford, 1962). I should point out, however, that
Edwards's successive demand curves would arise only for a business man
who persisted in being 'foolish' and who does not make the intelligent
anticipation that Harrod wishes to suppose; also that the time-scale need
certainly not stretch anything like as far as Harrod's long-run, which he
keeps referring to the construction of plants and the full establishment of
business from them. (Note, especially, my later remarks about 'cross-
entry', p. 78.)

Robinson's book right down to Harrod's suggested revision of imperfect competition theory. It may already have been noted that the passage from Machlup to which attention was called on page 41 itself involves the possibility of a significant interdependence of costs and revenues. I did not choose to dwell on the point then but, of course, it was an additional reason for the remark that the passage would seem to run counter to Machlup's line of argument. To the extent to which one line of development of the marginalist revolution has been to recognize developments which destroy the analytically necessary independence of cost curves and demand curves, it is another instance of realistic qualification eroding the validity of the analysis itself.

PART II
A CRITIQUE

A CRITIQUE

I. INTRODUCTION

In contrast to classical theory, modern (post-Chamberlin) theory has been preoccupied with demand questions even in the analysis of long-run situations. This may be seen as the natural consequence of theorists grappling successively with the increasing returns dilemma and with the oligopoly dilemma as briefly explained in Part I. Nevertheless, and paradoxical as it may seem, it is on the demand side that the modern development of the theory of the firm is most open to criticism. The critique presented in this half of the book, will, therefore, be especially directed at the analysis of demand functions. It will, however, be necessary to discuss a number of other factors whose consideration by orthodox theorists has tended, in my view, to be subordinated to a widely-felt methodological necessity that all analytical conclusions should conform to the Procrustean bed of marginalist-equilibrium equations.

No doubt, there could be a form of presentation which would carry the present critique along at one continuous analytical level. The difficulty as I see it, however is this: a critical handling of the marginalist-equilbrium method, at the broad level of general equilibrium which has often been thought appropriate to a presentation of marginal theory, or to the reconciliation of practical phenomena with it, must blur some important issues which are not adequately discussed in orthodox theory. The matter is therefore taken in several stages and, even though we traverse familiar ground, the next sub-section gives a synoptic view of the methodology which is to be criticized, as a kind of guiding thread.

2. MARGINALIST EQUILIBRIUM METHODOLOGY

$MR = MC$; $LRAR \ll LRAC$; $SRAR \ll SRAVC$;—these three equations together are the *passe-partout* of the modern orthodox theory of the firm.[1] The first decides the most profitable choice of output/sales open to the firm. MR, of course, is the marginal revenue from sales, and MC the marginal cost of producing the output sold, separate evaluations of these two functions being made for long- and short-run analyses. The second and third equations are used to determine whether or not the firm can continue to offer its most profitable output, in the long run, and in the short run, respectively.[2] In these equations LRAR denotes the long-run

[1] Equations of these types may be applied to other problems besides the determination of output, notably capital investment. Modern discussion of capital investment has, however, generally been remarkably untroubled by the cares which beset price/output theory. It must, of course, be the case that every investment decision incorporates some assumptions about the prices at which the resulting outputs will be sold and that many price/output decisions imply correlated capital investment. And so, as the Austrian school brilliantly demonstrated, price/output theory and capital investment theory are but two aspects of the same analysis which must be consistent as between them. In this present discussion we shall, however, confine ourselves to the price/output analysis which has been the chief preoccupation of marginalist equilibrium theory. (Elizabeth Brunner and I discussed orthodox investment theory in chapters i and x of our *Capital Development in Steel* and in a paper for the Oxford Economists' Research Group, in an unpublished symposium with Harrod and Champernowne, while we were members of that body. Ref. also A. Lamfalussy, *Investment and Growth in Mature Economies*, Macmillan, 1961.)

[2] I have elsewhere called attention to errors which can arise from the application of the third, short-run, equation. In abstract treatment, with labour, materials, and capital being taken as the three factors involved in production, labour and materials are typically taken as variable-cost factors, capital as *the* overhead-cost (non-variable cost) factor. It is not usual to allow for the fact that a considerable proportion of 'labour' may be overhead and this is probably why so little regard is paid to the possibility that overhead costs may involve the paying-out of current cash, if the business is to continue to exist even in the short run. This causes errors in the discussion of the short-term stability of industries. That body of abstract economic political conclusions which we call welfare analysis would also be affected by the recognition of this factor. No doubt, the welfare status of capital paying-out costs—'interest'—may be a matter for subtle dispute involving that dynamic progress of society which welfare theory tends to leave on one side. But most welfare theorists may be

price (= average revenue per unit) at which a firm may sell any given output, and LRAC, the long-run average cost per unit of that output. Similarly, SRAR is the short-run average revenue per unit of output for a given output, and SRAVC is the short-run average variable cost per unit of that output.

The time-scale: cost curves. Economists' references to time, in long- or short-run periods, are usually conceived with regard to output considerations and there is some lack of consonance between the time periods thus covered.[1] *Given* the prices of its factors of production and the state of technology, the *long-run* (average) cost curve, for example, will link the lowest (average) costs at which a firm can produce particular outputs, when it is completely free to vary its organization, its capital investment, and the employment of any other factor of production in whatever way it finds best. *Any* period of time which is too short for this is a 'short-run' period, and so a *short-run* (average) cost curve traces the lowest cost at which particular outputs can be produced at any time when the firm is not free thus to vary the whole of its production set-up (i.e. when it is constrained to remain organized to produce some particular long-run output). It follows that there is an infinite series of conceivable short-run cost curves, but abstract analysis usually runs in terms of *the* short-run cost curve and the long-run cost curve, the point of this analysis not being at all affected by the implicit arbitrariness with regard to the dating of short-run situations.[2]

presumed not to deny that labour has to be paid wages, nor that it should ordinarily be regarded both as withdrawable from any present employment and as having some potential social value (productivity) elsewhere. It would thus seem that theoretical advice advocating 'marginal-cost pricing' *tout court* in public industries may lead to error. This is not to say that there may not be good social grounds for running some public industries at a loss in some circumstances.

¹ See also the following page.
² Harrod in the 1930 paper reprinted as No. 3 of his *Economic Essays* hints strongly at a more extended classification of time periods starting from the rather short short-period end. This might have been followed up had economic analysis developed in a more realistic fashion, or had available statistics of industrial costs been developed to suit economic analysis rather than as by-products of administrative routines. To prevent

Demand curves. It should be noted that demand curves are instantaneous concepts in a sense in which cost curves are not. A demand curve traces the prices at which various quantities of a particular commodity can be sold, *given* the tastes and preferences of all potential buyers, the incomes of the latter, and the prices of all other products which these potential buyers may consider purchasing, whether or not these are substitutes in the ordinary sense. Although, therefore, one can conceive of *the* demand curve for a commodity at any particular time, to conceive of the prices which will be applicable at some future (longer-run) point of time involves rather more estimation than will be called for in the case of the corresponding cost curve. There is, moreover, not the same kind of analytical relationship, as between short- and long-run demand curves, as subsists between the corresponding cost curves (and most references to long-run demand curves are rather unsatisfying analytically, with loose reference to 'discounting' as solving the problem in some particular fashion presented as determinate[1]).

It is a real question, which will remain when later criticisms are considered, why we economists have been so ready to assume that long-run demand curves for individual businesses should have the same general shape as those which are conceived of as valid for instantaneous demand curves (and this is quite a separate point from that relating to the possible justification of concepts concerning the shapes of the latter to which we shall shortly be addressing ourselves).

The economic analyses which have been considered in the first part of this book have been concerned with two sorts of

misunderstandings following from my present summary of orthodox cost analysis, I should perhaps note that my own theory, as in *Manufacturing Business*, has developed a different view of short-run costs and the way in which business is organized to produce output in the short run, so that *on my definition* one gives up the 'envelope' relationship which necessarily subsists in orthodox analysis between the long-run cost curve for a firm and any one consistently defined system of short-run costs.

[1] Ref. M. J. Farrell, 'The Case Against the Imperfect Competition Theories', *Economic Journal*, 1951; and 'Deductive Systems and Empirical Generalizations in the Theory of the Firm', *Oxford Economic Papers* (New Series), 1952, p. 47, footnote 1.

demand curve. The *particular demand curve of a firm*, as I shall call it, is a 'monopolistic' kind of demand curve. The 'large-group' demand curves of Chamberlin and the analytically less-defined curves of Joan Robinson, Harrod (with the exception of a partial escape in his revision essay), Baumol, and Hicks fall into this class, as would any demand curve for a genuine isolated monopolist. We should similarly classify the more elastic, 'dd', demand curve of Chamberlin's small group (which traces the demand for an individual firm when it varies its prices but its rivals do not change theirs). The *share of the market demand curve*, as I shall call it, is that demand curve which Chamberlin ascribes to the individual firm in his small group when it and its rivals are imagined as changing their prices simultaneously. Fellner's demand curves belong formally to this class but their analytical definition is more ambiguous, varying from a simple Chamberlin small-group case (which gives rise to the 'joint maximization' which he stresses as characterizing his theory) to the uniquely-considered demand curve for a 'leader' as he varies his price and his 'followers' vary their prices in whatever way follows from their 'reactions' (in which case, as we have seen, the concept of 'joint maximization' breaks down).

Critical questions concerning firms' demand curves. In the following sub-sections we shall turn first to the question of the shapes of particular demand curves. We shall ask why they should be thought to be likely to exhibit, generally in a stable form which is kept unchanged for whole stretches of long-run analysis, the shapes which economic analysis has evolved to apply to the whole market for a commodity in perfect competition analysis, or the market for a commodity-class considered generally in monopolistic competition large-group analysis. We shall even question why this shape should be thought necessarily valid for a 'monopolist' just because he is the sole supplier to such a market (defined, of course, by a sufficient 'gap in the chain of substitutes', and the other niceties of strict monopoly analysis).

It may be thought obviously all right that share-of-the-market demand curves, in the strict formulation of

Chamberlin's most simple statement of his small-group case, should behave in the same fashion as would a demand curve for the whole group, if the products concerned were homogeneous commodities. We shall, however, later consider the possibility that some of the 'entry' considerations which cause me to doubt the validity of orthodox particular-demand-curve shapes cast shadows over these curves as well.

The general factors directly affecting demand-curve shapes which we have separately to consider in the critique which follows are the differentiation of firms' products, the effect of selling costs, and the scope for, and the effect of, new entry. It is noteworthy that orthodox marginalist theory has not constructed any special theory for retail trade (apart, that is, from the Hotelling-like analyses which have already been dealt with). Partly for this reason and partly because, at the present time, any probing into the roots of what has been said about retail trade seems capable of arousing passions which I should prefer not to rouse during the first stage of the presentation of my argument, we shall attempt an analytical separation of the consideration of retail trade from that of the marketing of commodities taken as at point of production. But, as a conclusion to our discussion of retail trade theory, economic considerations which have been adduced during the course of recent attacks on resale price maintenance will be used as a guide to the extent to which a common methodology may appear to underlie the professional consideration of this restrictive practice, in the United Kingdom at all events.

Other methodological issues. The separation of retail trade from manufacturing trade considerations means that the discussion of what is one important chain of activity will have to be broken up. I therefore give the warning that these points must be kept together in any summing up of the effect of this critique on the *general* validity of marginalist-equilibrium analysis (which, after all, is presented and used as a general system). General theorists will be found to move freely from the general analysis of firms and industry groups (in which, as we have seen, the shapes of firms' demand functions have been justified, if at all, by reference to 'Marshallian' commodity demand curves) to 'illustrations' of the argument from retail trade, without consideration of the extent to which simplifications, which may be valid enough for non-retail trade (and cost curves drawn up with regard to such simplifications) may or may not frustrate applications of general analysis to this area.

The principal 'simplification' which I have in mind is that which causes the theoretical firm generally to be analysed as though it were single-product. But this analytical measure deserves also to be dealt with in its own right, as does the treatment of business decisions as though they were taken at a single decision centre, with the related treatment of management as a monolithic sort of function.

It will be realized that we shall not generally come back to the criticism of particular models given in Part I.

At the end of this sub-section, I come back to the point that we are concerned with what is taught as, and is understood to be, a *general* system of analysis. Since most of the theoretical expositions of it with which we have been concerned have been long-run in their interest, or rather since for all of them the point from which our criticism starts is the long-run behaviour of demand, we also shall largely restrict ourselves to this end of the economic time-scale. It may be as well to point out that the long-run, so far as new entry is concerned, need not be a very long 'long-run' matter in any everyday sense. Even brand new businesses start their entry from the day they sell output from their factories, and it would be an extreme sort of delay that would involve even, say, three years to get to that position from the making of firm intentions to compete. For major classes of new entrant, the time-scale is much shorter and post-entry effectiveness is likely to be much sharper, as we shall see.

Nevertheless, the question of short-run behaviour will be considered at convenient points, although not in the detail which would be appropriate to the kind of positive exposition I have attempted elsewhere. For both long- and short-run questions, what is at issue is the validity of that equilibrium

F

concept which is the root of the orthodox system of analysis under criticism. At the end of the following section (A) we shall say something about the scope and character of an economics of the firm which has been purged of this concept.

(A) *Application to Non-retailer Firms*

This sectional heading is a reminder that we are criticizing first the orthodox theory of the firm in general and that the problem of retail trade will be considered separately.

3. THE SHAPES OF PARTICULAR DEMAND CURVES

The analytical uniformity of the particular demand functions which modern orthodox theorists have adopted, with finite-elasticity demand curves falling monotonously from left to right, raises, as already said, the question: why should the demand curve for a commodity which an individual business is producing in competition with others (or, whose market is formally open to the competition of others), be like that which is applied to the whole market for a commodity in a perfect-competition industry? We know, of course, that the validity of the latter usage depends on the commodity in question not having close substitution relationships with others. The formal answer to our question is that the products to which orthodox particular demand functions are considered to be applicable are thought to have their individual markets separated in just this sense.

Not every theorist has spelled out the basis for this, but the matter has really been left where it was settled by Chamberlin: the individual markets are conceived of as separated from one another by the buyers' preferences which each is thought to enjoy at any given pattern of prices, and there is therefore analytically a differentiation of the various products. It is not necessary that the products be different in fact. If they are actually identical in all relevant particulars, including their specifications, then the buyers' preferences which thus protect the individual markets must be considered to be irrational. If there are real differences between products, then

73

buyers' preferences *may* be rational, but there is still the possibility that they may be irrational in that they cause a greater degree of differentiation than the real differences would justify.

It would appear, however, that the analysis of the scope for, and the consequences of, genuine differentiation of products has been discouraged by the ease with which differentiation may be attributed to the irrationality of buyers,[1] and assumptions of irrationality have been more acceptable because of the apparent prevalence of differentiation. A reconsideration of these matters will lead to some of the major positive factors to be considered in this critique.

4. CAN DIFFERENTIATION PROVIDE A JUSTIFICATION?

Considering real, as distinct from fancied, differences between products, I suggest that any *general* theory should allow for, and perhaps should even postulate, a real differentiation of products as between suppliers. As will appear from our discussion of goodwill, the circumstance that a particular product is offered by this firm rather than that, even though each may offer goods otherwise identical, may well be grounds for it being separately regarded by buyers. Moreover, individual control over the circumstances of sale itself confers an ability to make such variations in other matters that physically identical goods may have different economic specifications when a sales transaction is regarded as a whole. And, of course, that same control must often give a supplier the ability to vary physical specifications themselves. The theory of the firm, and that wider theory of the industry which I believe should now return to economics, should therefore recognize this freedom to differentiate one's product.

[1] One remembers the zeal with which some economists propounded the enforced or artificially encouraged continuance of standardized consumer products after the war, the irrationality of consumers being thought to bar the exploitations of economies of scale whose realization was thought to be greatly affected. But this involved questionable ideas concerning scale economies whose discussion was itself inhibited by reasoning from, rather than to, the single-product models of industries which our modern methodology has encouraged.

A freedom to differentiate, however, is also a freedom to duplicate. To the extent to which there is freedom of entry to its market, any product, no matter how unique it may actually be, is exposed to the potential competition of products which can be made as identical with it as their suppliers choose—except, of course, for the inescapable difference that they will come from different sources and so bear, virtually, different brand names.[1]

Leaving aside the significance of brand names in themselves, which will take us into the questions of irrational preference and goodwill, to be discussed shortly, the conclusion would seem to be that the fact of actual differentiation of products is no reason for using the orthodox particular demand curves. These assume that, as a firm raises its price relatively to the prices at which others offer an identical product (or, in terms of the re-formulation of theory I have long argued for, relatively to the prices at which others *would* offer that product), although it will lose marginal custom as its price goes higher, it will still continue to enjoy its own market— and, as the orthodox long-run analyses go, given a stable relationship between its prices and those of others, this happy state of affairs will continue indefinitely. *Unless* we are to assume irrationality on the part of buyers, should we not assume that a price higher than would be quoted by would-be competitors must put the firm's 'own' market increasingly in peril from competition, and that the peril will be enhanced the higher its relative price is put?

If actual differentiation does not imply any necessary reduction of competitiveness, there is of course no reason to go on to deny the possibility, or rather to refuse to recognize the fact, of buyers' preferences as between sources of supply, even of identical products. This leads into the question of goodwill, which will be discussed subsequently. The prior question, however, is how far such preferences will

---

[1] The market for refrigerators would appear to show that, where consumers' requirements are met by simple standards, standardized products emerge even from different manufacturers. See also the interesting paper by N. H. Leyland, 'A Note on Price and Quality', *Oxford Economic Papers* (New Series), June 1949 (referring to lightweight bicycles).

be irrational in the sense that an identical product will continue to be taken at a higher price (e.g. merely because it has a different brand name).

5. SHOULD WE ASSUME IRRATIONALITY OF PREFERENCE?

Still bearing in mind that we are deferring the question of retail trade and the treatment of consumers' goods as sold to consumers, I shall deal shortly with irrationality in the rest of the business field. If economic analysis had not moved so easily into using 'consumers' as a general term for 'buyers', it would surely have recognized, long before I raised the matter in 1949, that we have to *presume* rationality wherever business men are buying goods for their own business use or for re-sale unbranded or under their own brand names. The very cost curves which are used so confidently in such models as we have been discussing in Part I and in economic analysis in general are explicitly constructed on the assumption that business men minimize their costs in a rational fashion. (Since I have discussed all this elsewhere, I shall not go into the positive side of the matter except to say that the purchasing function in actual businesses has its recognized importance. But its influence is also pervasive—for a firm whose buyer mistakenly buys less advantageously will have to sell to careful buyers in other businesses and the ground on which orthodox theory would assert that it might cover this with higher prices has already been removed from under the feet of the theorist.) I therefore assert that for this reason alone the theories which we are criticizing fail as *general* theories.

This matter, however, affects more than a mere corner of the economy, for sales of the kinds which we have been discussing make up a large proportion of total transactions. It is therefore surprising that our more recent general textbooks do not provide specifically for this area of the economy, and the plainly competitive theory which must be used to accommodate it. One would think that the reader might have been warned that much of the discussion of the imperfections of competition is without formal relevance to the longer-run analysis of business transactions as such.

The conclusion, surely, must be that, in the kind of market which we are discussing, a business must in the long run sell its product for no more than would be asked for a duplicate by any other business. If this does not lead to a neat marginalist determination of an equilibrium output, at least it entails that our analysis must run in terms of that *equilibrium of price*, as I have called it when arguing for this outcome. Falling demand curves for the long-run analyses of markets in the area which we are currently discussing would indeed seem to be 'out' as justifiable concepts.

The question of goodwill. The statement which has just been made does not mean that business men cannot make mistakes, that there cannot be careless buyers, etc. But we have indicated how a rational market will discipline businesses here. Nor does it mean that business men may not have preferences in the matter of continuing to deal with particular suppliers which they will exercise so long as this carries no penalty. Convenience of acquisition, and of accounting, as well as of use, may make a buyer prefer, other things being equal, to deal with one regular source rather than many. (Though the risks of having 'all the eggs in one basket' and the convenience of having regular direct knowledge of the actual invoice prices of other suppliers will equally often make for some spread of custom, provided that economy of buying is not affected.)

This means that short-run theory at all events should assume the fact of 'goodwill', provided that this is defined, as Marshall recognized it should be,[1] to be not without regard to price differences. We should therefore assume that the established business will enjoy buyers' preferences which will give it in the short run a stable market at the existing

---

[1] Ref. D. H. Macgregor, *Economic Thought and Policy*, pp. 39-40. (These remarks were later amplified by Macgregor in conversation about *Manufacturing Business*. He then summarized Marshall as frequently asserting that 'Goodwill was not without regard to price'.)

price, *provided that* this price be competitive against the offers of others.

6. THE QUESTION OF NEW-ENTRY COMPETITION

We have already implicitly raised the question of the effects of new entry competition. With the exception of parts of Fellner and the 'revision' essay of Harrod, the texts which we have been discussing follow the prevalent trend of orthodox theory in discussing 'industries' as though made up of a definite number of established firms, with new competitors having to come from businesses which are, not only new to the market which is being discussed, but also new businesses in the strict sense. It is therefore easy to think of existing businesses as being protected by the effects of the difficulties which such newcomers may be thought generally to face— the difficulties of capital finance, of acquiring brand reputations, and so on, with a tendency for us to associate these with the probability that newcomers will be rather small businesses and so suffer diseconomies on the cost side as well.

This theoretical bias is blown aside when one recognizes that new entrants may be businesses already established elsewhere. The facts of modern life show that it is from such businesses that new competition, in what for any reason their entrepreneurs may find to be attractive markets, is likely to be not only effective but also likely to operate relatively quickly with few of the impediments on which so much stress has been laid. This factor of the potential competition from existing businesses takes on explicit significance if we adopt the kind of model which postulates actual differentiation of products within an existing industry, as I think we should do. For the most immediate potential competitors are then businesses established in the same industry with all the facilities which that implies. I have called this extension of my concept of potential competition 'potential cross-entry'. Once recognized, instead of such markets (which are regarded by me as being differentiated no more than factually) being

analytically differentiated into little monopolies in the orthodox fashion, we are forced to regard each as subject to
strong competition of the kind we normally reserve for classical oligopoly conditions.

Fellner (as I have indicated) recognizes the possibility of
a wider view of new entry, but his discussion of the subject
suffers from his thinking in terms of 'big' new firms being
needed for successful entry[1] to a market where his own
'leader' is too easily contrasted with the other existing firms
as the large, low-cost firm, and the competitive strains between the larger businesses are not examined.[2] The writer
who has particularly addressed himself to the question of
entry, however, is Bain.

Bain's investigation. In his *Barriers to New Competition*
Bain took the important step of recognizing the importance
of potential as distinct from actual competition. His explicit
exclusion of the expansion of capacity by a firm already
within the industry put on one side the question of cross-
entry competition but that did not matter in itself since Bain
generally seems to assume competition within his industry.
But this may account for his not heeding sufficiently the position of businesses established already in other industries. In
the event, he concentrates on the costs of 'complete' new
plant and on such other matters as the difficulties of acquiring attractive brand-name positions. The empirical inquiries
which then dominate the book are preoccupied with the
difficulties of establishing new businesses in this restricted
sense. For this reason many of his conclusions are vitiated.

As Elizabeth Brunner has cogently pointed out, in comments specifically addressed to Bain's methodology, not only
may a newcomer to a market be already established elsewhere,
it may well be able to succeed at a relatively small size in its
new market because, e.g., it can use basic processes common
to some of its other goods, or spread other overheads by selling the new product through sales facilities which are used
in common with its other products. This latter point brings
up the question of the important potential competition from

---

[1] Ref. *op. cit.* p. 49.   [2] Cf. *op. cit. inter alia*, pp. 136-141.

customer businesses—if they come in, their supplying factory will not be at the usual arm's length from them. There will be economies through specializing production to their exclusive needs, and, paradoxically, in a trade with regular fluctuations they may get economies not open to independent suppliers through setting up relatively small plants which they can keep going on their 'base load' at much nearer full capacity than independent firms can achieve, whilst loading on to the suppliers of the 'peak load' needs the cost of the greater variability of output which is thereby induced. Many of the apparently settled oligopolies in the actual world, where a very few firms may seem to be highly protected by the large minimum scale of plant and high degree of technical know-how required, are in fact most open to competition from customers, often no less large and with quite adequate technical knowledge.[1]

7. THE RELEVANCE OF COST FUNCTIONS

Accepting the view that new entry is a much more pervasive phenomenon than much of the discussion of it would suggest, and that individual producers will be competing for the custom of rational buyers who will be very responsive to price differences, the forms of cost functions clearly become of independent importance. The highest price sustainable by an individual producer will be the lowest at which someone else will be willing to offer his commodity. In other words, the character of the individual demand function will depend upon the potential supply function of other producers, and the costs of additional supplies from them will depend upon their cost functions in the competitive conditions which have been argued for.

We have seen (p. 41) that Machlup made some such sug-

[1] Cf. Elizabeth Brunner, 'A Note on Potential Competition', *Journal of Industrial Economics*, 1961. Miss Brunner discusses an industrial application of Bain's model whose author did not treat the entry of *customer* businesses as an instance of the new entry competition into which he was explicitly inquiring.

gestion *mal à propos* what was explicitly a defence of formal marginal equilibrium analysis. It would seem possible that his acceptance of orthodox views of the shapes of cost functions was why Machlup did not apparently see just how much this particular suggestion, which was meant to brush aside a heretical approach to price, could lead to a view of prices which would swallow up the system he was contending for. If a business has a U-shaped long-run cost function, then its competition with regard to any one commodity at a given price will be of a strength which varies with its scale-position, ultimately weakening when it passes its optimum size, so that the sustaining of such competition at optimum strength will depend upon the entry of *other* businesses. The whole entry-competition question has therefore quite naturally been affected by orthodox ideas of cost functions.

Notions of relatively difficult entry-competition, in terms of disadvantageous smallness of newcomers and the advantageous economies of scale enjoyed by larger established businesses, which permeate so much modern discussion of the subject, clearly have one of their roots in these basic cost ideas. They also are rooted in an obstinate idea about the nature of equilibrium in non-perfect competition conditions which is a legacy from the earliest statements of the class of theory which we are criticizing—the idea that, in equilibrium, all established businesses will typically be on the left-hand side of their average cost curves, with the rate of fall of cost being determined by the low elasticity of the particular demand curve necessarily drawn as tangential to the average cost curve.

Since the purpose of this book is critical and not to put forward independently arguments for alternative theories, including that by myself (though since the latter has connexions with my present criticism I cannot avoid it coming tremblingly near the surface at times), we shall not go very far into this question of cost curves now. Recently developed empirical ideas on costs have, however, an obvious relevance to the present discussion.[1]

[1] See, especially, J. Johnston, *Statistical Cost Analysis* (McGraw Hill, 1960), where a good deal of other work is also discussed. We may note

To summarize the kind of conclusions which have been canvassed by myself and others: The principal change, so far as the short-run cost curves are concerned, is that the short-run average direct, or prime cost curve is conceived of as being horizontal, such cost being more or less constant over a wide range of output (which my theory discusses as the range of output for which a business is organized in the short run). Long-run cost curves, which have the most immediate relevance to our present discussion, are conceived as having what I have called the reverse-J shape—fairly steep falls in average costs for increases of scale in the neighbourhood of really small firms, and with the rate of fall progressively slackening off with size relatively soon in terms of the stable structure of an industry. In terms of such long-run cost curves it follows that firms of relatively moderate size may survive in effective competition with much larger businesses.[1] It also would follow that, if a business finds it profitable to enter into competition with a product at a given level of price, it will sustain that competition continuously so long as that level continues.

Harrod, in his revision of imperfect competition theory, accepted these empirical ideas about cost functions but he inserted directly into his models only the conclusions about short-run average direct costs. He allowed, as we have seen, the conclusions about long-run costs to come in only indirectly, through the anticipations of business men concerning the long-run elastic demand curve which would apply to

that the theoretical relevance of the conclusions is enhanced by their being apparently commonly held independently by practical business men, and so, even if these ideas are believed to be erroneous, they should be assumed to enter into the expectations which will determine business conduct.

[1] Because one important criticism which I make of the modern theoretical orthodoxy is that it has caused ideas of industrial structure to atrophy, I note that these ideas about the behaviour of costs taken in conjunction with a recognition of the importance of paying-out overhead costs, form important elements in my theory of stable industrial structures as both relevant to the competitive industrial set-up for any one individual class of product and to the general competition between businesses operating similar processes. Ref., *inter alia*, my 'Limites Économiques à la Dimension et à la Croissance des Entreprises Individuelles', *Revue Économique*, No. 1, January 1956.

their individual product if they sustained too high a price. He wished to retain the conventional form of demand curve, as a separate explicit element in his analysis, because he saw it as his function to get as much as possible of what he regarded as an empirical account of price formation into the forms of imperfect competition analysis without abandoning the 'classical' structure of that analysis. I have already spelled out the objection to this which I put to Harrod at the time, as a failure to develop the analytical connexion between demand curves and cost curves which I considered to be entailed by the very generalizations which Harrod was accepting, and which, as I demonstrated, my theories presumed.

8. THE SHAPES OF SHARE-OF-THE-MARKET DEMAND CURVES

In the preceding pages, we have taken our fences on the side of models where real differentiation of products is prevalent. Conventional demand curves of finite elasticity have been rejected, following the conclusion that the kinds of buyers with whom we have been concerned must all be rational in their preferences, and also having regard to the pervasiveness of new-entry competition, which must be reinforced by the revision of ideas concerning costs which has been put forward. These conditions, it has been suggested, lead to an analytical equilibrium of price, but not of output, the latter being determined by goodwill so long as the individual business remains fully competitive (in the given conditions of technological and product inventions—to break out of the static into the real world to which goodwill belongs). But, given actual differentiation of product, the impact of potential competition, from insiders at present producing different products as well as outsiders, has brought us, as will have been realized, to an analysis of the individual product market which is *explicitly* oligopolistic in form. Oligopoly thus takes to itself what orthodoxy has tried to keep separate as competitive price theory. (Indeed, as foreshadowed on

84 ON COMPETITION IN ECONOMIC THEORY

page 16, any real monopoly, not artificially protected from new entry competition, must also be approached in terms of this potential competition analysis.)

In reaching this conclusion I have, of course, already constructed an implicit destructive criticism of those share-of-the-market demand curves which Chamberlin evolved as part of the framework within which demand for the products of his small group operated, and which Fellner took over as the basic concept in his joint-profit maximization leadership-cartel theory. For such demand curves have analytical validity *only* for a group which is closed to new entry (and even then, their use in stable-equilibrium analysis requires special assumptions about collusion, which themselves are made more feasible by orthodox ideas of cost functions whose U-shapes so necessarily weaken the apparent force of *intra*-group competition).

According to the present critique, one might very well have *actual* oligopoly, but *potential* competition removes the ring fence which is necessary for the playing of classical and neo-classical games. Our troubles over the diversely constructed demand curves of oligopolists indeed disappear; and in their place we should have a different kind of demand function. The special connotations of oligopoly in equilibrium theory disappear.

This is not to deny that oligopolistic disequilibria can occur, or that, if such conditions do come about, cumulative mutual price competition may be pictured in terms of firms being driven down the patterns of their shares of the over-all market for the competitive group of commodities. But the traditional disequilibria of oligopoly theory came about in an attempt to construct a theory for equilibrium conditions. Any analysis of the kinds of short-run disequilibria which may in fact occur requires recourse to a theory of industrial structure. Although I myself have published the beginnings of such a theory, this is not a topic which comes up directly in a criticism of theories from which genuine industrial ideas are absent. A theory of industrial structure must, indeed, get entangled with the flux and stresses of the real world which orthodox construc-

tions of static marginalist equilibrium theories have kept
outside their analyses. ('Realistic' side references by orthodox
theorists have too often been sources of confusion rather than
genuine illustrations of their theories.)

9. SELLING COSTS

It will probably have become clear already that the criticism of this section of the book has destroyed the relevance of
the orthodox concept of selling costs to the analysis of the
sector of the economy which we have been considering. The
orthodox concept does not involve mere physical delivery
costs, or the costs of providing the information for buyers
which is a condition of maintaining a market at all, but rather
the expenditure on persuasion in order to bend demand progressively towards one, the real qualities of the goods for the
buyer not having to be affected. Selling costs as thus defined,
if analysed in terms of lasting effects, belong to a theoretical
world of irrational consumers.

The allegedly similar effects of mere delivery costs have
been disposed of in the criticism of Hotelling-like constructions which was given in Part I. Information gives rise to no
such analytical effects. The question of the relevance of orthodox kinds of selling costs, notably advertising, to consumer
markets will be considered in section B of this part. In any
theoretical model for the rational kind of economy which
should be conceded for the present section, there can be no
lasting advantage from mere persuasion, which it would be
misleading to see as capable of extending the market by shifting the demand curves outward whilst, at the same time, reducing their elasticities; and thus it should not be seen as
giving lasting protection against assaults by other firms on
the basis of straight price competition. The doubts on this
account which modern orthodoxy has tended to cast on the
efficacy of such competition as a matter of *general* theory
are therefore unjustified. To go farther than we have
gone into the matter of actual selling costs in non-retail

sectors of industry would take us gratuitously into positive theorizing.

10. OLIGOPSONY

The economies of the operation of base-load plants in customer-industries, referred to when we discussed Bain's work on entry, can sometimes be one fulcrum for the exercise of oligopsony power—the power of influencing suppliers' prices which large buyers may have through their ability to concentrate their patronage. This is a matter which needs to be analysed in terms of relevant industrial structures and the economic effects of the exercise of oligopsony power may be quite different according to the cost-function characteristics of the two levels of industry concerned. The kinds of theory which we are reviewing are, as we have already said, innocent of structural problems. Those which run in terms of the equilibria of isolated firms can develop no analysis of the effects of oligopsony at all. Otherwise, the matter is left simply as a question of the effects of bargaining power, and the attention is concentrated on the effects on prices in an analysis where the unvaried demand functions which are employed assume away all structural consequences.

Some further discussion of this will be relevant when we consider the application of orthodox theory to retail trade. In my view, some of the discussion of the effects of resale price maintenance has been vitiated by non-recognition of the possible effects of retailer-oligopsony on the whole manufacturing/distribution complex in which resale price maintenance exercises its restrictive power.

11. OTHER ISSUES: THE SINGLE-PRODUCT FIRM

We turn now, from the criticism of orthodox theory in terms of the economic position of the individual firm as such theory chooses to think of it, to two issues which are concerned with the firm itself as it is brought into the analysis. The first of these is the analysis of the firm in terms of the production and sale of a single product. Classical usage has made this traditional in economics. It may be thought especially curious, however, that the question of the propriety of this procedure has been raised by orthodox theorists as a point against *other* kinds of theories rather than as a prelude to self-examination.[1] This traditional usage is in fact more easily justified with regard to classical, or Marshallian, competitive theory than it is with regard to the body of atomistic equilibrium theory which, from its origins, has been concerned with analytical details at the level only of the firm in order to settle the behaviour of the individual business to an extent which did not arise for the older macro-orientated theories.[2]

Orthodox analysis, as we have seen, runs in terms of demand functions which are conceived as varying significantly in character from product to product. It also embodies cost curves whose shapes will similarly vary, so that quite complex questions arise concerning the effects of the combination of products—especially if the nature of the product mix has to be thought of as varying with the scale of the firm as a whole, e.g. relative to its industry in general. This latter question in turn throws us back to the demand function, for it is conceivable that there is some complementarity between products which analysis ought to take into account yet which the very use of the orthodox demand functions precludes—e.g. consider the possibility that a large firm because it has to serve the market as a whole may have to produce all major classes of the industry's products, whereas a smaller business may specialize. An analysis of the orthodox kind, which proceeds from analyses in terms of single products to conclusions which invite or thrust upon us applications to 'firms' as we

[1] See E. A. G. Robinson, 'The Pricing of Manufactured Products', *Economic Journal*, 1950, p. 774, n. 1; and Joan Robinson, *Collected Economic Papers*, vol. 2, *op. cit.* p. 234, n. 2.
[2] I have discussed this issue with regard to older theories and resolved it at the level of the individual firm in terms of my own theory in 'Industrial Analysis in Economics', *op. cit.* p. 14, n. 2 above.

G

know them, should surely have considered how the combination of products might affect the relative positions of businesses, and whether such an effect was systematically related to the structure of the industry or of its markets.

All this clearly affects realistic discussion, in the context of marginalist equilibrium theory, of such matters as the 'efficiency' of smaller businesses (and that not merely as along a single-product cost curve) and the scope for new entry, and provides yet another reason for comment on the absence of structural analysis in orthodox theory. Structure in recent times has been left as a question for the 'applied' economist and has resolved itself into mere statistical analysis of the proportionate importance of the larger businesses in administratively defined industries, to which theoretical economists feel free to make loose allusions derived from simple monopolistic analysis. More recently, preoccupation with growth questions has led to the development of ideas, derived from the kind of analysis which we are criticizing, of businesses as inner-directed, growing by straining at their own boot straps. Confrontation with statistics from which 'growth' firms cannot be clearly identified may lead to a consciousness of effects of competition which the micro-equilibrium emphasis of the economist's training does little to elucidate.[1]

12. THE MONOLITHIC FIRM

This critique has already shown how the scope for that 'competitiveness' which is the central preoccupation of orthodox economists may be obscured by the constructions which abstract models have employed. This obfuscation, however, spreads from the very heart of the analysis, from the concept of the firm itself. A 'firm' is conceived as a single entity, competing as an economic atom with other atoms, and picking its

[1] Ref. I. M. D. Little, 'Higgledy-Piggledy Growth', *Bulletin of the Oxford University Institute of Statistics*, 1962. For earlier statistical work of a similar interest see H. Secrist, *The Triumph of Mediocrity in Business* (Bureau of Business Research, Northwestern University, 1935).

course of action with regard to the effects on its profitability conceived as a whole. This concentration of interest makes considerable sense when one considers, say, the long-run investment decisions where sectional proposals have to be ironed out 'at top level' with a regard to the business as a whole, but even there it can cause one to pay insufficient attention to the processes whereby the proposals got to the top and even to details of the ironing-out process which have relation to individual activities within and of the firm.[1] It will be clear from this statement of the matter, however, how much this monolithic analysis abstracts from what happens in the business, and how that is directed, as a going concern.

A multi-product firm may be organized in separate departments, plants, or divisions, often with their own links to the sales side, so that there is much scope for both product and process to exert pressure in the interest of their own competitive position. Yet another analytical division of the orthodox monolith may be made in recognition of the impact of diversity of outlook and interest as between buying, production, and sales (and, outside the vision of static theory, research, and development). Such analytical diversities of interests within the firm may also be seen as supplemented by the pressures of the individual interests of management personnel, judged from above, at any subordinate stage, by their achievements in their individual tasks which often are measured by a sales/profit yardstick built into reporting procedures.

Since orthodox analysis is innocent of this matter, it is impossible to discuss it at all without raising positive points on which fresh analysis should be hung. I have myself pointed out the scope which there is, not only for the cost-reducing development within a business of what I have called 'internal competition', but also for the outwards-directed pressures of competition which are direct consequences of these internal

---

[1] This is why Andrews' and Brunner's discussion of the capital investment policy of United Steel Companies after the war was preluded not only by a discussion of technical processes but by the earlier history of each of the branches—ref. *Capital Development in Steel* (Basil Blackwell, Oxford, 1951).

competitive forces.[1] As in biology, some theory of internal process and structure might be expected to be useful to the understanding of the performance of an economic entity. The activities and interests to which I have referred are, clearly, economic matters in economic organizations. Ought we not to encourage a hardier presumption that there is work for an economist to do within the firm than is displayed by contemporary trends, which would rather hand over the area to sociologists, behaviourists, and others whose fundamental scientific interests are different?

13. THE ISSUE OF MICRO-EQUILIBRIUM ITSELF

Is this book so far but 'treason from within'? In professional contacts I have become aware of some feeling that, in adopting so critical an attitude towards the micro-equilibrium methodology, I am asking my colleagues to give up a birthright on which our science has prospered; one valued friend has put it that this is our legacy from the classical economists as far back as Ricardo. Plainly this is not so (and our science has not notably prospered by the investment of our 'legacy' in the field of industrial economics). Marshall, at least, refused to be committed to the full static equilibrium of the firm in the analyses which had bearing on the problems of industries. And, until him, the other progenitors of classical economics, whether in England or on the Continent, were concerned with the more general problems of the economy as a whole, with only the broadest reference to industries as operational elements. In the resulting analyses, any propositions which explicitly or implicitly bore on the equilibria of individual firms were but incidental to the interests of our classical predecessors.

Nothing in my critique indicates that we should give up the principle of substitution—that principle of economy

---

[1] I have made further reference to 'internal competition' in 'Competition in the Modern Economy', *Competitive Aspects of Oil Operations*, ed. Sell (Institute of Petroleum, London, 1958).

which does indeed link us with the primal cells of economic reasoning. We can, moreover, still retain ideas of a firm in balance, a sort of equilibrium; but this would be a balance with its environment, the industrial environment, defined with reference to the processes and products which would give the most direct possible generation of competition with the firm in question, and changes in which would have the most immediate implications for it. As I see it, a theory of this kind could still be made to *look* consistent with marginal analysis, but the balance of the firm would *not* be determinate within our orthodox equations, except in a Pickwickian sense. The limiting inequalities whichthe marginal equations would become would merely indicate the competitively determined price which it would not pay the firm to vary; its output/scale would be indeterminate by reference to the marginal equations and should be seen as decided by that goodwill whose analysis would involve dynamic considerations. However, to give up all notions which involve our thinking of individual firms as at all times masters of their individual destinies seems to me to be the gateway to a revivified theory of the industry.

However we formulate it, our analysis could be only explicitly static; the terms in which it would be constructed would have dynamic implications, themselves the proper subject of analysis. One does not get a dynamic theory merely by writing time into static analysis. We should thus hope for a framework for further work on individual industries of a truly analytical kind, in which relevant factors in the internal structure of the firm would be linked with the analysis of the external circumstances in the industry, where again, a structured theory would tie on to the analysis of the economy as a whole. And, from the other end, macro theories could be linked with classifications of industries which would be operationally significant.

It is true also that, in our efforts to understand and predict the behaviour of the entities of the theory of the firm, we ought to be looking rather beyond the present towards longer-run trends. But why should we have expected that we could say much about actuality with a theory which assumes that, in all the flux and uncertainty of the real world, individual businesses may be treated as though they were at rest?

To follow this theme would take me too far from our subject—and involve the therefore-irrelevant representation to the reader of the models of *Manufacturing Business* and other writings of my own. But I must register my belief that the ending of marginalist static equilibrium at the level of the firm as the seat of a sovereign *general* theory would free us to use our economists' tools on change and chance in the real world in a way that our supposed 'legacy' has denied to us. I count it as a real obstacle to dynamic thinking that this particular static theory has encouraged us to make *a priori* generalizations about the behaviour of businesses without any feeling that it was part of the job of the theorist to get nearer the apparently muddy and confused real world of business management.[1]

Ending this section, something may be said by way of consolation to those who may think that, in giving up the nicely precise idea of equilibrium as we understand it, economics would lose that quality which marks it off from the less fortunate sister social sciences, which lack the theoretical foundations of the kind in which economists are trained. The physical sciences have had to face just such a methodological break during this century. The laws which are applied to assemblies

---

[1] It puzzles me that my divergence from equilibriumistic theory should have taken so long to be discussed. (Ref. Romney Robinson, 'The Economics of Disequilibrium Price', *Quarterly Journal of Economics*, 1961.) D. H. Robertson dealt with it as rather an aside, that he thought I held this position (ref. his *Economic Commentaries*, chapter i, p. 37). But a recognition of this should have prevented his identification of my positive results with those of Marshall, to which, as he indicated in correspondence, he attached much importance. The real puzzle is that, in view of this misidentification of me, he did not feel called upon to explain what we all took at the time as an authoritative recognition by him of Marshall's representative firm as the equivalent of Pigou's equilibrium firm (since I in fact was taking such a different view). That recognition (ref. Robertson, 'Increasing Returns and the Representative Firm: The Trees of the Forest', *Economic Journal*, 1930) was a step which had serious consequences not only in the development of the *Economic Journal* controversy but in shunting the thinking of English economists away from what Marshall was really concerned to do with the representative firm idea which he had thus presented with, as it seemed, strange lack of clarity for so accomplished a mathematician.

of many atoms were discovered not to be applicable at the level of the atom. Accepting this, physicists have not forced their macro theory at the atomic level, nor have they given up research at that level in despair.

To be sure, we economists could not face complete uncertainty of analysis of *our* 'atoms' with equanimity, for individual firms bulk large in our universe. That is, of course, no reason for retaining a misleading methodology but, accepting the critique which has been put forward, we could still hope to say a lot about our atomic entities. We could hope to predict their behaviours in a general way with the help of a revived industrial theory which would enable us to be fairly precise about the circumstances bearing most closely on the behaviour of firms. We should not be surprised that static micro-equilibrium analysis should turn out to be invalid, for the individual firm itself is so very much in a changing world and its behaviour is an adaptation to that fact. The point, however, remains that the most important forces would appear to be analysable at what we call the industry level.

(B) *Application to Retailer Firms*

14. GENERAL REMARKS

In this section, we consider the *applicability* rather than actual *application* of the orthodox system of marginalist equilibrium analysis to the retail end of the economy. There are plenty of 'aside' references to retailers and retailing in the Chamberlinian and Robinsonian literature, but no authoritative theoretical texts which handle retailing for its own sake after due consideration of the relevant applicability of the constituents of the parent theories—the demand and cost functions which we have discussed.

Because I know them best I shall refer to three specialist writings which, although they were published in England, have achieved international status. Margaret Hall's chapter on economic analysis in her study of distributive trading[1] is a spelling out of orthodox theory which does not go further than is necessary for her immediate purpose, but it will be found, I think, that the present critique has direct application there. Smith might originally have been classified fairly simply as a Chamberlinian, despite the strains which his realistic approach imposed on his theoretical structure, but the chapter on 'pure economics' in his revised edition[2] is now a very useful presentation of relevant categories of topics within the ambit of theory, which would appear generally to have been influenced by Lewis, rather than a formulation of a unified model, and it does not lend itself to systematic criticism.

[1] Margaret Hall, *Distributive Trading* (Hutchinson's University Library, N.D.). Lady Hall has of course carried on working in this field, witness the monumental work, *Distribution in Great Britain and North America*, by Margaret Hall, John Knapp, and Christopher Winsten (Oxford University Press, 1961). She has not, however, yet returned to the question of the theory of the firm in retail trade.
[2] Henry Smith, *Retail Distribution, A Critical Analysis* (Oxford University Press, 1948).

Lewis's well-known essay on retail trade,[1] of course, starts outside the genealogy with which we are concerned, although a good many details of his partial-equilibrium approach would be susceptible to my critique. The main line of the essay however, as indicated earlier, is rooted in the Hotelling system of analysis which has already been criticized. From this point of time it seems a pity that the apparent cogency of this approach prevented Lewis from working out an independent model using important ideas, notably that of the shopping centre and of a general rationality of the consumer, which he rather worked in as modifications of the general model so that monopolistic analysis comes to pieces in his hands, as it seems.

Whilst thus making reference to retail trade literature, I should like to call attention to McClelland's essays.[2] McClelland has a rare combination of qualifications, as an academic economist with his high-level entrepreneurial responsibility in retailing. He has not yet addressed himself to the task of building any general model, but the details of his essays on retailing would seem to me to be more comfortable within a model which was consistent with the present critique than within any orthodox model.[3]

In effect, so far as the applicability of relevant general economic theory is concerned, the Hotelling kind of approach has been the only alternative to that based on Chamberlin. In my judgement, Chamberlinian ideas have had the wider influence and have permeated the thinking of economists as being of ready application to retailing. This view would seem to be borne out by the statements, and the reticences, of pro-

[1] Op. cit. p. 13 above.
[2] W. G. McClelland, Studies in Retailing (Basil Blackwell, Oxford, 1963).
[3] I instance the stress on the shop and firm rather than on the individual commodity as the unit of analysis for price formation. Readers of these essays and of the second part of Friday's and my Fair Trade may be interested to ponder why, when we agree on so many details, McClelland should reach such a different balance in some of his conclusions. His views on the competitive rôle of manufacturers' brands are a case in point. That he has the experience of having to sell such brands is no answer since it is clear that the policy which he advocates here would tend to bring him considerable relief from that 'obligation'.

fessional economists during the controversy over resale price maintenance in England. It is therefore the Chamberlinian system of analysis that we shall be concerned with for the rest of this sub-section. Although we shall proceed in an abstract fashion without further reference to literature, at the end of this section I shall summarize the arguments which were made in favour of a ban on 'r.p.m.', and show how vulnerable they are to my criticism of the Chamberlinian model.

15. THE ORTHODOX 'COMMODITY' APPROACH

The orthodox approach to any industry is in terms of single commodities. Although such theoretical simplification may turn out all right for broad practical purposes in non-retail trade theory, provided that the theoretical model be of a non-orthodox kind (see p. 78, n. 2), and although it may be useful even for orthodox models, when we are thinking about the economy as a whole, to reason in terms of isolated commodities is, I shall suggest, not so easily defensible when one is discussing firms in retail trade. It seems desirable, however, before coming to that criticism to question the application of orthodox commodity demand curves in themselves.

The question of 'services'. Despite the fact that the retailer often 'does' something to his commodities, economists find themselves constrained to regard retailing as fundamentally a service trade. Nevertheless, leaving out such trades as dry-cleaning (and even there one may find it is sometimes rational to regard the same suit back from different cleaners as a different commodity!), I agree with Holton that retail purchasers typically buy *commodities*.[1] Certainly, if we want to chain our analysis of manufacturing economics on to the retail stage, then it is much more convenient to keep our reasoning in terms of the commodities which left the manufacturing stage, following them, as the questions in which we may be interested lead us, through a relevant classification of retail

[1] Richard H. Holton, 'Price Discrimination at Retail: the Supermarket Case', *Journal of Industrial Economics*, October 1957.

outlets, considering the analytical peculiarities of each separately. Those 'peculiarities' will be found to be very much bound up with the characteristic 'service', in the widest sense, of the individual retail outlets.

It is the, difficult-to-justify, carry-over of the single-commodity approach of orthodox theory into the analysis of retail trade itself which obliges those using such a theory to refer to retail services as though they were analytically separate commodities sold alongside the commodity-good proper, and thus one gets forced into a separable analysis of services which, but for this constraint, we should see to be inappropriate.

The complex of services which a shop offers is much more than the services which are thus separated for analytical purposes.[1] Moreover, the separable—marginal—costs can be only a part of the total costs which should be ascribed to the provision of the services that economists ordinarily do separately distinguish. The simplest analytical procedure, when we are concerned with retail trade as such would therefore seem to be to discuss *shops* in terms of the kinds of service which they offer and start the matter from there.

Since we shall later come on to the question of the shop as an entity in orthodox theory, I shall discuss the demand functions for individual commodities in retail trade without further reference to services in this sub-section. In any discussion of the shapes of demand functions for individual commodities, however, it is necessary first to get over the hurdle of a presumed irrationality of the buyer.

The question of 'rationality'. The question whether buyers are to be regarded as rational or irrational in general theoretical models of retail trade cannot be dealt with so simply as the similar question concerning trade buyers was dealt with in the previous section of this critique. In retail trade theory, we are dealing with ordinary consumers buying a multitude of commodities and, as it might be thought, with only amateur qualifications as buyers.

---

[1] This emerges plainly from pp. 2-16 of Smith, *op. cit.*, and on p. 19 (e.g. the discussion of fresh and other fruit) Smith gets near a bundling of services together in a proper classification of commodities.

There is, moreover, the question of advertising, whose very forms suggest how consumers are influenced by factors other than information which bears strictly upon the aspects of commodities which are relevant to rational choice. It is easy to take all this as proving in itself that consumers are not rational in their choices, but I shall suggest that advertising has been considered only against a grossly simplified background which itself stems from the type of theory which I am criticizing. We shall, therefore, probably find it helpful to defer the question of advertising until we have considered other matters.

Pending the further hearing on advertising, then, we consider the question of the rationality of consumer choice apart from any corruption induced by sales promotion. Although this would be a very difficult question indeed if we were trying to settle it as universally or invariably to be positively applied, it is helpful, for our present purposes, to remember that an approach to retail trade in terms of a *general* theory may fairly be criticized on the basis of the feasibility of *its* generality. The question we are aiming at is, of course, whether theory is justified in assuming falling demand curves for individual commodities as sold in retail trade; and, since theory has so largely been concerned with structural matters affecting retail trade (e.g. the growth of supermarkets and the positions of independent shopkeepers), we are concerned with the longer-run validity of such demand curves.

Further, our approach would have to be very different if we were considering, say, a large rural state in which small urban centres were distributed remotely rather like nebulae in the universe. A developed country such as England, however, has a predominant urban economy in which shops do not characteristically compete in isolated locations but in shopping centres, and these again have closely woven inter-connexions and are competitive one with another. Too much of apparently realistic reference to retail trade has been content to draw contrasts between the large chain store organization and the little corner shop in the suburbs of a town or the small general shop in a village.

The validity of a *general* theoretical approach, such as that which we are criticizing, must therefore be affected by its applicability to the urban complexes within which most retail buyers move around. With such chaining-up of competition, are we, then, justified in using models with falling demand curves for individual commodities at their point of sale by the individual retailer? The answer to that question must be No, if consumers exercise their choices rationally.

'Rationality' gives rise to interpretative problems in other contexts, but in economics this quality has a fairly clear, technical, meaning—a man is rational if he chooses whichever alternative costs less, taking into account all aspects other than cost which affect the value in use to him of each alternative. It is an unfair gloss on this usage to say that an irrational consumer is one who persists in choosing the dearer commodity after an economist has demonstrated that another is cheaper, but there is a methodological point in it for economists. One of the things we have to guard against is that we may not recognize rational conduct when we meet it.

Our guide to the relevant alternatives in any situation can only be our analysis of that situation, and we necessarily simplify actual or possible actual situations in order to be able to reason about them. Our orthodox analyses of consumers' choices issue in demand functions in which a consumer is conceived as demanding a definite quantity at a given price. In such a function, 'price' may be taken to include any other 'costs of acquisition' and has to be considered to be adjusted in other ways so as to preserve the functional comparability of any situations we may be considering apart from 'actual' price. In any formulation of the demand function care is, of course, taken to clarify these *ceteris paribus* reservations with regard to price.

Nevertheless, we are bound to go on describing relevant choices, as an economic situation changes, in terms of 'prices', and it may be relevant here that our demand functions are basically short-run in their definition (other prices, incomes, etc., being taken as constant). This aspect of our analyses is relevant to most of the discussion of profit maximization,

which we take as the rule for rational conduct on the part of
a producer. The effect of our own systems of analyses is, I
believe, a tendency to equate rationality with chasing the
'cheapest dollar' wherever it may be, and without giving
much explicit consideration to any factor other than price.
However that may be, I have been impressed by the number
of occasions in the course of my studies of businesses when,
following up a line of conduct which would ordinarily be
treated as irrational on the face of it (and which I myself in
the early days have treated as irrational), I have nevertheless
found when I got more insight into the circumstances affecting it that the conduct had its economic rationality.

Some of the reasons why I myself would now argue that
we should assume longer-run rationality even in retail markets are, frankly, empirical in nature. I would adduce an
apparent tendency towards similar gross margins for similar
classes of shops in urban markets. I am also impressed by the
fact that practical managements, as well as academic specialists in retail marketing, use such gross margins when they
discuss particular markets and businesses within them. After
my industrial experience I would also pay some attention to
the statements of seasoned retailers that they assume that
their customers are price- and quality-conscious. The habits
and customs which consumers appear to have developed with
regard to their purchase of different classes of commodity also
seem to me to point the same way. However, as I shall make
plain, it is not necessary to go as far as I myself do with regard
to the tendency towards rationality on the part of consumers
in order to have to accept an economic analysis which is substantially that which we should make if we were to assume
this rationality.

The leaven in the lump. It seems that one very simple consideration will suffice to establish how far from necessary it is
to require a universal rationality of consumer choice: A minority of rational buyers at any time would suffice to make it
profitable for the urban retailer, in the matter of the quality
of his goods and the prices which he puts on them, not to behave very differently from how he would behave *if* consumers

generally were rational. I myself call this 'the Ward-Perkins point' because the first time that I came across it as a formal proposition was in the course of an essay by the late Neville Ward-Perkins, then my pupil at New College. It seemed then, and it still seems to me, to be a very powerful point indeed.

Let there be, for example, at any one time only 10 per cent of consumers who are rational in their choices, weighing up quality against price, and price against quality, on the basis of the real value which they find in continued purchase. (As against this minimal proposition, would one really say that in terms of longer-run tendencies one would expect only one in ten of consumers to choose rationally?) A mere 10 per cent of the demand in an urban area would be large compared with the sizes of individual shops. Many individual shops, therefore, will find that, in relation to their own possible range of sizes, there is a very large potential market sensitive to price differences. Surely this high elasticity of demand at the margin as between identical commodities would favour a general presumption of parity of prices as between shops in any one district (i.e. systematic cost-factors being taken into account), without need to take account of the distribution of preferences as between shops? At least, it surely should do so apart from the considerations arising from the 'argument of the market basket', to categorize a factor which is discussed below. This latter reservation concerns the point that consumers in a shop should not be thought of as weighing up all commodities *individually*, however rational they are. Subject to that further point, our present conclusion taken by itself, is a sufficient objection to the use of partial demand curves of finite elasticity when we are considering the *general* theory of the sale of identical individual commodities by different retailers.

The effects of purchasing habits: multiple purchases. The theoretical system which we are criticizing is also vitiated in the case of retail trade by two further considerations which arise from shopping habits, to which insufficient attention is paid in most of the extensions of orthodox marginalist equilibrium theory to retail trade, or to supposed problems in that area which have largely been identified in the light of the theory concerned. Whatever may be thought of any particular positive theory of retail trade which may be built on such ideas, their recognition has destructive, negative, consequences for orthodox theory.

The first of these considerations is the habit of general shopping expeditions, and the habit otherwise of covering a number of purchases when one goes out with particular purchases in mind. As this makes clear, however, some goods, e.g., of high value or bought infrequently, may be the object of special visits to the shops or be the nucleus of a wider foray. Many, however, are habitually bought as but part of a regular, general shopping trip.

These two kinds of shopping expedition play their part in my explanation in *Fair Trade* of the competitive rôles of different kinds of shop. I here take only two—but very important—cases, for the sake of having a simple model which we can use as the basis for specific criticisms later:[1] I instance 'specialist' shops (offering a choice of their kind of merchandise, and commonly located near each other because of the attractions to buyers of having wider comparisons within reach) and 'general' shops (specializing in ranges of diverse goods from which buyers regularly select a number on any one trip, and offering also whatever else they find it attractive to their customers to hold in stock—so that these may well offer narrower ranges of choice in particular departments than will 'specialists', and will naturally tend to concentrate on the more popular lines).

The 'rational' buyers going regularly to particular shops must be considered as *not* necessarily achieving a nice balance between the 'marginal utility' of any *individual* good and that of the money they lay out on it. In the 'general' shops, their satisfactions with their purchases should surely be conceived in terms of the *groupings* of commodities which they normally

---

[1] Experience has shown that it may be helpful to warn the reader to notice in what follows that the term 'general' has a particular significance, so that, e.g., supermarkets fall within its application, and indeed, in the analysis of current changes in retail trade in England, may be thought a leading example.

H

expect to buy in an individual shop when they contemplate shopping expeditions. Once in the shop on any one occasion, the customer should be thought of as conveniently getting as many as possible of the goods on his current 'list', subject to the influence of general notions of the value he will ordinarily get 'across the shopping basket', modified by any expectations he may have of there being sufficient gain from making particular purchases elsewhere.[1]

The commodities of the 'specialist' shops, however, will stand on their own so far as those shops are concerned. Their expected prices must be attractive enough to bring buyers to them for their commodities specifically, and they must always expect to share the trade in their goods with general shops stocking narrower lines of them, where buyers are not affected by any desire to be able to make more extensive comparisons or have no expectations of price-gains from them.

'*Impulse*' *buying*. To approach consumers' choices in retail trade in terms of the isolated demand curves for precisely defined individual commodities, as orthodox theory has to do, gives rise to other distortions apart from the inattention to the phenomenon of the shopping basket to which we have just referred. One of the most serious of these is associated with the concept of 'impulse' buying, and our discussion of it is intended to cover the second aspect of shopping habits to which I wish to refer.

It is, surely, rational to go shopping for *a* blouse, *a* shirt, *a* pair of socks, for example (or even 'something nice for tea'), and to decide the precise style, make, etc. (and thus to settle on the particular commodity the choice of which orthodox theory has to treat as determinate *before* rational analysis can be developed according to its ideas), only whilst actually shop-

---

[1] Realistically, 'he' should be 'she' for many kinds of purchase. I have discussed the economics of the 'basket' in my part of *Fair Trade*, but see also the article by Robert D. Entenberg and A. James Boness, 'On the idea of a Market', to be published in the *Journal of Industrial Economics*, autumn 1964. For another sector of retail trade, there are also interesting generalizations in Entenberg's *The Changing Competitive Position of Department Stores in the United States by Merchandise Lines* (University of Pittsburgh, 1961).

ping. It is no less rational, it seems to me, to decide in this
way even what kind of commodity to buy; for example, to
decide to have an evening out, to reject that idea after inspec-
tion of what the local cinemas have to offer, and then to buy
a book to take for one's entertainment at home. The only
term which orthodox theorists have found for such optative
purchasing is 'impulse buying'. The evident undertones of
an essential irrationality in this term are amplified in theoretical discussion of such habits. I suggest the terms *discretionary
buying* and *discretional purchase* as likely to convey the essential point for theoretical analysis without the sense of irrita-
tion which the pejorative 'impulse' carries quite naturally
for the theorist who cannot handle the phenomena concerned
within his analytical framework.

It will be evident how wide is the scope of discretionary
buying, and therefore how important it is that analytical account should be taken of it. It must be expected to affect the
precise generation of demand for a very large number of goods
and whole lines of trade must be greatly affected by it. Non-
recognition of the nature and scope of discretionary buying
probably accounts for the practically non-existent recognition of the *active* rôle of stocks in orthodox retail trade
theory.

The rôle of stocks. Without going at all fully into the analysis of discretional purchases, it should, indeed, be clear that
precisely which commodities, and how much of them, will be
bought at any one time will depend upon the character of the
stocks which are available as well as their distribution in the
shops which consumers visit or consider visiting. A corollary
of this is that the whole trade of the specialist shops must be
dependent upon their continuing to offer a sufficient range of
goods in their stocks for people normally to choose to come
to them rather than select from what is available in the general
shops. Any significant switching away from them of the sales
of their more popular bread-and-butter lines will, whatever
other advantages may be thought to flow from it, reduce the
basis on which they can afford to carry their stocks of other
items. Granted that general shops will necessarily limit the

numbers of brands which they stock in particular lines of trade,[1] it can also be seen that the survival of smaller manufacturers' brands, and even of the minor brands of larger manufacturers, may depend entirely upon the fortunes of the specialist shops whose trade may be a large proportion of their total turnover.

Coming to the general point at issue, it follows that the orthodox presentation of the market for a commodity in retail trade in terms simply of demand and cost functions at a single outlet is doubly misleading. First, the stock function needs to be introduced explicitly into the analysis (and this point means in itself that the analytical separateness of the demand and cost functions is illusory; they are not independent of each other). Secondly, when this is done, one can with propriety no longer theorize in terms of the isolated shop demand functions of orthodox theory; since different types of shops play a different part here, and since they will be differently affected by any changes affecting the commodity which are being analysed, one has once more to bring into the analysis the whole question of industrial structure which modern theory has so strikingly ignored since the Chamberlinian revolution.

Entry considerations. On the basis of the detailed points already made, we may deal more shortly with other matters so far as the present critique is concerned. The fact that one

---

[1] On this point, whose significance for the overall competitiveness of retail trade has been entirely overlooked in recent controversy, see McClelland, *op. cit.* p. 117, where its force is slightly muted by the earlier reference to the extension of the general range of goods carried by supermarkets. The reader should start with the jams mentioned lower down the page and then think of the third- and fourth-ranking brands of domestic appliances and other commodities whose sales possibilities would be so seriously affected by the structural changes in retail trade, which McClelland discusses without further consideration of this point. It is not a guarantee of increased overall competitiveness that we should come down to two, or three, independent national brands, as would appear very likely to happen, as we note in the text, in important lines of trade as a consequence of the ban on resale price maintenance destroying the market for these brands in other shops (which provides the only springboard from which the manufacturer of a minor brand—who need not be a minor manufacturer—can create the wider acceptance of his product needed for him to develop successful competition with the major brands and force his way even into supermarkets).

of these is the question of new entry competition will empha-
size how substantial is their potential analytical importance.

Still thinking in terms of individual commodities, and for-
getting for the moment the heavy implicit criticism of this
orthodox approach which other considerations have developed, it will be clear that it must be assumed that new competitors can very easily take up the sale of any particular
commodity. All that is necessary for a shop to compete with
others in this respect is for it to add the commodity in question to its line of goods, and the marginal costs of so doing
will be low in relation to a shop's average costs (assuming,
for the moment, that it makes economic sense to suppose that
this latter category of costs *can* be referred back to individual
commodities), for reasons which will be summarized when we
consider shops as the legitimate entities of retail trade analysis.

The oligopoly factor. It will also have become apparent that,
commodity by commodity, granted there is a sufficient proportion of rational buyers (and we have already seen that this
need not be at all a large proportion), retail competition
should be seen as working through a network of oligopolies
which probably should be conceived as specifiable from the
point of view of any individual consumer. The impasse of
oligopoly must therefore itself frustrate any application of the
demand/cost-curve models which underlie many judgements
concerning retailing. Since Chamberlin himself has increasingly stressed the chaining-up of oligopolies as a characteristic of retail trade, it is surprising that there has been so little
explicit general recognition of the frustrations which this
must bring here for orthodox marginalist equilibrium theory.
Theorists have gone on regardless using determinate market
analysis of the individual firm.

Conclusions regarding demand functions. My chief conclusion is that, looking to factors affecting individual commodities alone as we have done in this sub-section so far, the fact
that purchases are so frequently combined in the shop, and
the probability of oligopoly relationships between the markets of individual shops, alike, make it illegitimate to analyse
the retail trade in a commodity in terms of individual demand

curves referred to the individual retailers who sell them. We have, moreover, in the dependence of demand upon stocks, uncovered one reason why equilibrium analysis, based on the confrontation of what purport to be independent individual demand and cost curves, is not justifiable. Beyond this, if we conceive that the *total* demand for any class of commodity or its costs of supply can be affected by the stocks carried by any particular class of retailer, then the demand realized by any *one* shop, and basic elements in its cost functions, will be affected by the general structure of trade in that class of commodity.

The discussion so far suggests that the individual shop, rather than the individual commodity on which modern theory has concentrated, is the valid entity for the economic analysis of retail trade. When we turn to consider shops as analytical subjects we shall indeed discover yet more serious reasons for criticizing any analysis of retail trade purporting to discuss the generation of demand and the determination of price, which is seen in terms of demand curves and cost curves for individual commodities.

If one should, however, persist in using demand functions referred to individual commodities at the point of sale by the individual retailer, then, at the very least, one should regard the individual shop's demand curve in this case as being likely to be very elastic indeed for a shop in an urban area—that much, at least, must follow from consideration of the effects of the rational buyers in an oligopolistic network of retailers. This is especially so if the analyst is discussing such matters as changes in the structure of retail trade due, say, to the development of a new type of shop, for these are essentially longer-run matters, and any 'frictions' of the short-run must be presumed to be smoothed away. If, however, one were to seek for an explanation of the levels of such very elastic curves one would, *via* the competition which must be assumed to produce them, be forced into the questions about the determination of individual costs to competing retailers which would leave one frustrated by the difficulty of isolating such cost functions.

The fallacy of marginal supply. Before turning to shops

themselves as economic entities, there is one other fallacy in many orthodox discussions of retail trade which should be brought to light. In the underlying kind of economic analysis, the persistence of a business in long-run situations is seen to imply that it manages to cover its total costs by its receipts. We shall take a look at that proposition later; meanwhile we should note that a consequence of it, in models constructed in terms of individual commodities, is that the longer-run offering of that commodity for sale is likewise regarded as dependent upon all retailers involved being able to cover their costs by their prices. Any persistent level of price, therefore, is easily described as necessarily 'covering' the costs of marginal retailers. This is the fallacy of the marginal supply.

It is a fallacy, in the present context, if only for the reason that the buying habits of consumers must be seen to entail that the cost of stocking any one commodity may be justified, in the complex of the individual shop, not only by its own price and the total demand for it but also by reason of the effects which the terms on which it is offered may have on the demand for *other* commodities. It follows that a shop may continue to offer a commodity even if the direct receipts from it do not suffice to cover the costs of keeping it on offer. (Even this, of course, assumes that the shopkeeper can, in such circumstances, be clear about what precisely are the costs of his trading in one commodity [although his long-run costs must on any notion be higher than his invoice costs of buying it]. We shall later see that this is a doubtful proposition.) It follows also that it is of doubtful legitimacy to speak of shops as clearly showing different levels of *efficiency* in their dealings with but one commodity, when the reasoning was in terms of average gross margins for *shops* which have been analysed as if they are relatable to individual commodities.

16. THE ECONOMICS OF THE SHOP

So far we have been devoting attention to orthodox analysis of the retail market for a single commodity in terms of the demand functions which are formally applicable only to the individual shop's market for that commodity. (They are in fact normally presented only for *an*—or *the*—individual shop.) This procedure involves the treatment of the whole of the market for a commodity as though it were but a collection of analytically separate individual shop markets. My criticism has not supported this method but has rather pointed towards an analytical concatenation of markets at the shop level.

Now that we consider the theory of the retail firm itself, it is convenient to make a general point of some importance: orthodox theorists have not really been concerned with retail trade in the broadest sense and have not included any general analysis of retail firms, in the sense of *organizations* of shops. The general theory of the firm has sometimes been extended to cover a firm of more than a single plant, but in the retail trade area its application runs in terms of the individual shop. Even though I am not propounding positive theory for its own interest (and so shall not go far into the interesting question of the market implications of various kinds of organization), my criticisms will occasionally force us outside the limits of the orthodox treatment, notably when considering the question of the effects of oligopsony. This question has not received much attention in theoretical discussion of retail trade. Policy judgements made without regard to it may be wrong, e.g. assessments of the active competitiveness of kinds of shop as though only their 'efficiency' as retailers were involved.

A comparison of the subject-matter of the present sub-section with that of sub-section 15 leads to the point that the use of conventional single-product models of retail firms in orthodox analysis causes the position of the retail firm to be pictured in terms of the very same demand (and cost) functions that appear in the analysis of the retail commodity. It may appear, at first sight, that all we are doing as between these two sub-sections is simply to look at the same analytical model from two different viewpoints. To put the matter in that way, however, emphasizes that we are drawing a distinction which modern methodology avoids in principle; it is, nevertheless, a necessary distinction and one which has to be made in the methodological appraisal of any industrial theory.

The fact that the distinction is not made in the theory we are discussing means that a good deal of my criticism of the individual commodity demand functions, in sub-section 15, is also valid when one considers the application of the orthodox theory of the firm to the shop of retail trade. Indeed, in earlier drafts of the present sub-section, I found that a parallel treatment of its subject-matter involved a re-pointing of previous criticisms which might well have seemed mere repetition to any reader whose training should lead him to take single-product models for granted. We are not nowadays trained to draw that distinction between the commodity and the firm which, as I have said, should always be made (but, when it is made, of course some single-product models may be found to pass the test of their suitability for the general analyses in which they were used).

In sub-section 15, therefore, I adopted a quite separate treatment of commodity analysis on the demand side; but I dealt with the individual commodity cost functions rather *en passant*, just because they seem to lack application to retail trade (however much they may be valid simplifications in the theory of manufacturing industry). I thought it more useful to consider details affecting cost functions as part of the background of the present re-examination of the analysis of the retail firm. Of course, it follows that much that will now have to be said about costs will have direct critical application to the analysis of the market for an individual commodity in connexion with the use of any cost functions there.

In this sub-section, it has seemed convenient not to work inside a continuous discussion of the orthodox demand/cost-curve construction, but to raise topics which cut across that territory in several directions. Nevertheless, recalling a quotation from a favourite poem by Yeats—'Feet to the Rising and Setting may run, they always beat on the same small stone'— my criticism will bear continually on the construction whose methodology I object to. What we shall be discussing, in

effect, will be a number of fallacies engendered by the orthodox use of equilibrium methodology.

The two major points which are relevant here are the legitimacy of studying retail trade in terms of single-product firm
models, and the validity of a system of analysis which runs
in terms of the individual shop considered in the abstract on
its own. Both of these engender fallacies in the analysis of
'efficiency' in the context of retail trade. The second also involves the lack of consideration of the inter-relationships between kinds of shop which give a structure to retail trade in
practice, and which orthodox theory can handle only in rather
flabby 'asides', as though all shops were analytically on a par
and evaluable in terms of the same demand/cost-curve diagram. Discussion of this latter point will bring us sharply
against the fallacy which the single-product shop models engender—that of discussing the generation of the whole retail
demand for a commodity as though it were merely a matter of
short-run prices in individual shops and were not affected by
the general system of retail trade in which it must develop,
and by longer-run repercussions within that system.

The single-product model of the shop. I have said that orthodox single-product models of the firm may conceivably be
legitimate simplifications in the analysis of industrial activity;
the criticisms which have already been made of individual demand functions, however, suggest that it is illegitimate to use
such 'conflated' models in retail trade theory.

Such a model treats the aggregate of demand which a shop
might enjoy, for all the goods which it may have on offer, as
though it can be approximated by the demand curve for a
single commodity. In particular, the system of theory under
criticism discusses both the total demand which a shop might
continue to enjoy as the long-run consequences of some particular price policy, and the long-run effects of changes in
that price policy, as though these could be read off a particular sort of demand curve, of the kind which economic theory
has evolved (as in Marshall's *Principles*, Book III) for the
whole market of a homogeneous commodity.

That the total demand for the firm's commodities will be

the sum of the demands for its separate commodities is true enough, obviously; but the point is that, in the case of a retail shop, such an aggregation is not the addition of independent quantities. The stocks and price policy for one good must affect the demand for the others in the ways which we have already discussed. There is no reason to assume, even for a given shop in a given set of external circumstances (and the prevalence of oligopoly may well mean that changes within and by the shop will cause the external circumstances themselves to change), that the product mix, and the interactions of the stocks and demands for the individual goods in the mix, will remain unchanged, even assuming relative prices to remain unchanged or to change in a regular fashion as the shop extends its 'demand', by whatever means that may be achieved. (Reflexion will show that the latter kind of regularity of price behaviour is an essential condition of there being any analytical value in a demand curve of the kind under criticism.) However, it is unlikely that any such changes in other dimensions of demand *would* leave relative prices unchanged. Similar considerations obviously affect the behaviour of the aggregate of costs which orthodox theory also treats as though it could be represented by the cost curves which have been evolved to illustrate the cost functions applicable to a single commodity.

Leaving on one side the question of relative individual price changes, it is true that, if one takes as the unit of sale not the individual commodities but the combination of purchases which individual buyers, in settled external conditions, make within any one shop, then one *might* simplify the demand side of the analysis of that shop into a single demand function. But then we should have to abandon the types of models with their finite elasticity Marshallian kind of demand curves; for the criticisms which have already been made of individual commodity demand functions indicate not only that it would be wrong to give such a composite function the finite elasticity of Marshallian demand curves, but also that it should be regarded as very elastic in the neighbourhood of the prices at which competing retailers would offer similar combinations of commodities.

This discussion may conveniently be followed by brief remarks on the questions of new entry and on the shapes of
individual shop cost functions. It will be seen that consideration of these matters reinforces the suggestions we have just
made about the elasticity of any legitimate kind of aggregate
demand function, since they point towards the long-run sus-
tenance of competition at near-constant levels of the prices
of the relevant product combinations, postulated for legitimate aggregation. It follows that the 'modified' aggregate
demand curve which has been tentatively conceded could not
be used for the nice analysis of *alternative* price policies at
the individual shop level which is the essence of the orthodox
approach to retail trade.

The question of entry. I do not think it is a controversial
point that retail trade is an easy-entry class of industry and
therefore shall not labour it. This general conclusion is reinforced by the comparatively large turnover of enterprise
which is always going on. Easy exit being thus combined with
easy entry is a reason for applying longer-run rather than
shorter-run analyses to retail trade.

The turnover of enterprises, however, suggests that there
is a fallacy in orthodox methods of long-run analysis which
assume that the constant supply of entrepreneurial talent and
capital, which would be necessary for a long-run equilibrium,
will be maintained only if the actual rewards which they
achieve will cover the normal costs of the marginal sector of
firms. The phenomena referred to suggest that the marginal
sector is covered at a loss. This *fallacy of the marginal supplier*
is exactly analogous to the fallacy of the marginal supply
which was demonstrated in sub-section 15. This point is
taken up again on page 136.

The shapes of cost functions and the question of oligopsony.
It will already have been made clear that the question of the
form of the cost function which is attributable to the supply of
the *individual* commodity is meaningless in retail trade, in so
far as there is such complementarity between the commodities offered by any one shop that part of the costs of some
commodities at least must be analysed as incurred in order to

get the benefits of the sale of *other* commodities. It must also
be said that the importance of fixed costs, and particularly of
those which are general to the establishment, entails that the
costs which are allocable to the supply of the individual commodities, apart from invoice costs, are but a small proportion
of total costs. The general importance at any one time of
fixed costs and, within these, of paying-out costs (see p.66, n. 2),
must be seen as giving the individual shop a considerable incentive to increase its turnover in whatever way it can at a
net gain over not much more than invoice costs, provided
that other sales are not prejudiced. This characteristic of
short-run cost curves therefore contributes to the evident
tendency towards multi-product competition in retail trade; it
also implies that there is none of that tendency towards the
long-run relationship between individual marginal total costs
and marginal revenues which the single-product analyses of
orthodox theory so confidently assume.

Analysis of the long-run cost function is complicated by
the question of the variability of product-mix which has already been referred to. Leaving that on one side, i.e. even
assuming that the commodity-mix is constant, there are technical difficulties in the formulation of conclusions about the
shapes of long-run cost functions for the individual shop,
largely resulting from the importance of rents, into which we
do not need to go for present purposes.[1] What can be said is
that the ease of establishing other outlets and the absence of
diseconomies from growing by adding to the number of outlets (see the following paragraph)—regardless of the conclusions that might be reached about the economies or diseconо-
mies of increased scale of the individual shop—mean that the
cost side of the retail business is not to be analysed as causing
any slackening in the incentives to competition because of the
increase in the size of the firm.

So far as concerns changes in the costs of the retail organization, conceived as resulting from its growth in terms of the
numbers of outlets under its control, it is unfortunate that so

[1] Some consideration of this is given in Note C, and on pp. 45-6, of
Fair Trade (*op. cit.*).

much of the available statistical work on retail costs has been carried out in terms only of individual shops or establishments within organizations. I myself would accept the views which I have found generally held by practical retailers that, apart from the benefits which might be obtained on the purchasing side and which raise the question of oligopsony discussed later, multi-store retail firms do not make further substantial economies once they have gone beyond a moderate size in terms of the number of units. Even purchasing economies seem to taper off till one reaches the scale of a large national business able to command reductions in prices because the purchasing power which it can swing around is large even in relation to the capacity of important suppliers in its lines of business. The point at which either sort of economy will taper off will, of course, depend on the commodity concerned and the sector of retail trade. Within any one type of trade, however, it would seem to me likely that both types of economies taper off sufficiently—subject to the exceptional position of the really large business whose very scale sets some limits on the trades in which it can act as a unitary organization—for us to accept that organizations which are moderate in size from the point of view of capital and management problems will generally be able to maintain a very competitive position with larger businesses. No doubt one day this impressionistic view will be capable of being tested statistically, but although I would theorize on its basis, if only because of the light which it sheds on observable phenomena in retail trade, it need be regarded here only as an attempt to provide the sort of generalization which would rationalize the confidence with which I find, say, the chief manager of a local and not very large chain of supermarkets regarding the competitive efforts of large national rivals in his area.

A point for our general criticism in all this, of course, is that the orthodox uniform U-cost curve suggests a restriction of competition, due to dis-economies of scale, *from within the industry* which does seem to give a false impression of retail trade.

Reverting to the question of the economies of buying which

businesses may get as they increase in size, there clearly has not been enough discussion of the effects of the oligopsony power of retail businesses at the largest end of the size scale, where, as I have said, there would appear to be special buying advantages. Analysis so far has not adequately discussed the possibility that, through exercizing their power of transferring large blocks of purchasing power, such organizations may in effect be able to 'export' part of the costs, which on a long-run analysis would arise from dealing with them, into the accounts of smaller competitors.

Looking at the actual retail trade situation, it may well be that oligopsony gains help to offset actual dis-economies of size for the really large retail organization. It may well also be the case that the gains from buying power, although they have tended to become notable, even with resale price maintenance, in the case of the purchase by large retailers of other people's branded goods, will often be more substantial in the case of products bought in large quantities to be sold as 'own brands'. It will have become clear that I think it probable that these oligopsonistic reductions in buying prices at the top end of the retail size scale will not imply corresponding economies in the production and selling costs of the suppliers who find that they have to allow them. To the extent that this is so, the larger retail firms enjoy adventitious advantages in their competition with other smaller retail businesses.

Unstructured atomism. By now, the details of this critique will have indicated the major reasons why I think it unfortunate that the apparently natural extension to the retail trade area of the modern marginalistic equilibrium theory of the firm, has led to retail trade analyses which themselves run in simple terms of a single-shop model.

Such constructions are blind from birth. It does not need a very experienced eye to pick out in the retail trade scene classes of shop which stand out as significantly different from the economic point of view. Economists, even when using the kind of approach which I criticize, freely refer to one class of shop (e.g. the supermarket, seen as a revolutionary development or innovation) or another (e.g. the small corner grocery shop, to name the example commonly given as at the other extreme). Since they themselves seize on what they regard as large differences between classes of shops, it is extraordinary that no one had developed an economic analysis of the individual classes which are thus distinguished, if only to see how far what are thought to be obvious generalizations about the ways in which the shops of any one class compete with those of another are valid. To have done so, of course, would at once have brought out the difficulty of sustaining these generalizations in terms of the costs of selling individual commodities.

Our own discussion will have already made it clear that it may be useful to distinguish kinds of shopping centres when assessing the competitive rôle of individual shops, and that kinds of shops should be distinguished more generally, as with the 'specialist' and 'general' shops referred to on pp. 103-4. (see also pp. 132-4). Even this partial view of a structure of retail trade has brought out the point that shops may differ in the extent to which they are accessible to the frequent visits of large numbers of people, in the extent of their appeal by their range of commodities or by their range of choice within a commodity class, and so on. We have also seen something of the positive functions of the stocks which do not appear in the orthodox single-shop diagrams.

What one has to remember is how often consumers will see themselves as having the choice of the same commodities in different shops. Orthodox reference to 'services' not only bends thought in the direction of monopolistic competition analyses of retail trade, but it also obscures, as I have suggested, just what the majority of services do—they characterize the shop and the way it fits into a competitive retail trade complex, in which the consumer is being tempted to buy particular commodities *here* rather than elsewhere, and have little obvious relevance to his choices between commodities.

The peculiar treatment of services in ordinary analysis can be seen as a direct consequence of a single-product model which has to be interpreted in terms of the single functions relating to an individual commodity. Each shop therefore is treated indiscriminately as though it were selling the same commodity, and to throw the difference between classes of shops into some other characteristic is the only way in which those differences can be brought into analysis. But since the 'services' of shops actually involve their stocks and the diversity of the commodities which they sell and other things besides the particular kinds of services which economists ordinarily distinguish, it naturally leads to error to throw all differences into a single kind of characteristic which is then called 'services'.

Retail trade should be analysed as a structured industry. The very differences between shops have their part to play in the question of the total market demand for a commodity which must therefore be analysed as a whole. The orthodox approach to retail demand fragments the total unanalytically by reason of the models which never can consider more than the isolated demand of the individual shop and compounds this error by the consequential neglect of the ways in which classes of shops make their distinctive contributions to aggregate demand.

When one reflects on the shops specializing in particular types of commodity, even if one has not had the experience of looking at them through the eyes of a manufacturer planning his distribution, surely it must be clear that they *might* play a more direct rôle in the gestation and in the maintenance of demand, for all their individual specialist groups of commodities, than the 'general' shops which merely stock the more popular lines? Not only does the range of the latter tend to be narrower, and these can reduce their range or even drop the goods altogether without damaging the foundation of their trade, but also the effects of the so-called 'impulse' buying must be to engender a more diverse kind of demand in the general shops; in the specialist shops, on the other hand, it can work only to strengthen the demand for the kinds of goods sold by them. When, therefore, critics propose changes which will enable the general shops to increase their share of the more popular lines in which the specialists also deal, it can be only the myopia of orthodox atomistic analysis

I

which prevents them from seeing that they must also consider the likely effect on the total demand for any particular
class of commodity concerned.

Further reflexion on 'services'. Having referred to the ways
in which specialist shops may contribute to the generation of
demand through the 'service' of their wider range of stocks
(and on page 106 I showed how this class of shop may have
important effects through encouraging the continued competition of manufacturers' brands which fall below third or
even second place in the national league table for the particular type of product involved), I should like to return to this
question of the way in which orthodox theory approaches the
services of retail traders.

We tend too easily to regard the 'services' of a shop only
in terms of, so to speak, utilities which are bought with the
individual good, almost as though they were part of the individual shop's specifications for the good in the state in which
it sells it. It is normal to instance such things as credit, delivery, luxury appointments, repairs, and after-sales services in
general. There is no doubt that such things are either small
beer in the overall costs of the shop or they tend to be charged
for separately anyway. The costs of fitted carpets are minute
compared with the charge for rent in a department store. The
costs of wrapping are normally at least as high in the kinds of
shops ordinarily discussed as though they sold 'without service'. Even for furniture it is apparently rare for delivery
costs to add up to more than 2 per cent of turnover. After-
sales guarantees are normally at the cost of the manufacturer.
There is also the point that the consumer may get repairs
done more cheaply in the specialist shops with large turnovers
in the line of goods concerned than he would if he had to pay
for the service on a genuinely independent basis, whether
in manufacturers' own separate service branches or otherwise.

What we have tended to neglect completely in retail trade
analysis is the important kind of services which shops give
before sales, by which they virtually create their demand
themselves. Again, to come back to an earlier point, the main-

tenance of stocks is one of the most important services of this
kind and its cost is one of the ingredients making up the gross
margin which can be suggested to be large in comparison with
what a shop would need simply to sell the more popular lines,
so long as their present overall level of demand continues,
without lining the shelves with stocks to meet the emergen-
cies which at present are met by the stocks available from
genuine stockists. It is very easy for people to use the services
of the stocks (and the advice) of the specialists, when comparison shopping, in order to decide what they will buy and
then to buy that elsewhere, when they are ready to buy it, in
the course of a shopping trip to a different kind of shop. In
present circumstances such specialists survive on what people
do buy from them, untroubled by the probability of loss-
leader competition elsewhere.

The fallacy of 'efficiency'. The unstructured approach to
retail trade in terms of the single firm not only leads to a fallacious kind of approach to the very generation of demand,
which is presented as so patly available to any individual shop
that it may be 'read' from a demand curve where all that
apparently matters is the price in that shop. In my opinion
it also leads, taken into account with the single-product
methodology of the analysis, to a fallacious handling of the
general question of 'efficiency' in retail trade. Everything is
handled in terms of the individual retailer's 'costs' which
would be relevant to the simple diagrams in which the basic
analysis is conducted but whose relevance to the actual world
is, as we have seen, not so clear. Certainly an argument which
starts from individual retailers cost's and related ideas of
their 'efficiencies' takes a good many things for granted.

First, it is assumed that because a new form of retail trade
shows larger gross margins this is a sign of greater efficiency
which will be sustained at the end of the day when the 'revolution' has fully developed. Second, from the overall margins
for shops or classes of shops there is a tendency to jump to
costs for the individual product, and it is thought that the
shops which are assumed generally to have larger gross margins will have lower costs not only generally, but also in the

sale of individual commodities. The further related assumption is made that retailers sell individual goods at their individual cost—*plus*; instead of the assumption which seems more nearly in accord with experience, that they will try to get as high a price for each good as they think they can sustain against competition, bearing in mind the benefit which they may get in higher prices for other goods, if they can attract customers with low prices on this one; and such a set-up will be the more sustainable if the cut-price good is not one which is important in the trade of nearby competitors of their own kind; therefore we may take it that it is not very important to them; it follows that the commodity will not make an important contribution to their overall 'efficiency' and one may therefore not read back from the latter to their 'efficiency' in selling this particular good (e.g. no-one would assert that Nescafé was a major part of sales in supermarkets—its cut-price sales were used in order to get customers away from the other kinds of grocers).

From this it is an easy step to assume that the specialist retailer who cannot match the general shop's cut in the price of one of his own major goods is as less efficient as he would be if the real world were made up of single-product shops and all were competing on the basis of just covering their competitive full costs on these individual goods. I have already referred to the way in which the gains from oligopsony may be fallaciously interpreted as due to efficiency and shown how classifying it in that way leads to neglecting the overall effect on social costs and prices. Consumers of other goods or of the same goods bought elsewhere (from shops for which there is no ground for any assertion that they use up more 'scarce resources' in the distribution of these goods than the supermarkets do), may contribute (by reason of their having to bear some proportion of the costs of suppliers to supermarkets unjustifiably) to the presumed-to-be lower prices resulting from the presumed 'efficiency' which the oligopsonists are presumed to 'pass on'.

This erroneous approach to retail trade has developed because in the original statements of the modern marginal equilibrium theory of the firm retail trade seemed to be such a 'natural'. Conclusions which, as we have seen, have no necessary validity have been pressed home in retail trade, partly because we are all consumers of the goods it sells and so have a *prima facie* interest in cut prices, and partly because the application of such a theory to manufacturing industry does not seem so simple. In manufacturing one comes up against 'real' costs of production; any consideration of these in retail trade is avoided by reference to gross margins only; the margins of retail trade are then easily seen as *merely* a payment for a service, and a good deal of the costs of giving that service are represented by profits or by rents. Both of these rather lack immediate appeal for the critic; the former because one cannot be sure that profits are as low as they ought to be and would be if the world were perfectly competitive; the latter because, as every economist knows, rent is a cost to the private individual but is determined by prices when analysed from the social point of view.

Before turning to our final discussion of resale price maintenance, which is the area where ideas derived from orthodox theory would seem to have had their most striking practical effect, I return to the consideration of advertising which was adjourned on page 99.

17. THE EFFECTS OF ADVERTISING

As was said in the first part of this book, advertising is a subject which was not handled analytically until the advent of Chamberlin's theory and it was one of the creative effects of his work that economists began to think that they could handle selling costs of this kind. There has been no further development in the analysis of advertising although there have been a number of signs that specialist theorists have gradually become aware that some questions are unsolved even within the settled framework of analysis, e.g. the determination of the level of expenditure on advertising in the small-group oligopoly case. It is here to be argued that the

I 2

discussion of advertising in terms of the orthodox theory I am criticizing has been affected by the errors which we are beginning to see as systematic in that theory. It appears to me, therefore, that this also is an area where future theoretical progress depends upon the abandonment of this method of analysis.

Advertising is apparently fitted neatly into the static marginalist equilibrium strait jacket on the basis of its persuasive function. The successful persuasion of consumers is interpreted as causing the shifting of the individual firm's demand curve to the right, the curve at the same time becoming less elastic than it would have been without advertising. This gives, in the large-group case, a long-term equilibrium in which prices are higher on account of the expenditure on selling costs, consumers paying more because they have been persuaded to value commodities more highly. In an oligopolistic small-group setting, the treatment of advertising is, of course, as indeterminate as the analysis of price without it. The conclusions which are possible within the large-group case have, however, had effect on professional attitudes (e.g. the 'wastes of advertising'), and implicit acceptance of collusion in the analysis of oligopoly makes it possible for these attitudes to be expressed in comments on the advertising expenditures of oligopolistic industries, with collusion itself resolving the analytical indeterminacy of expenditure on advertising.

The general conclusion of this Critique is plain: if the given, taken for granted, demand curves of orthodox theory may not be used for the kind of analyses in which we use them, away goes any orthodox structure within which advertising may be assessed. In other words, if my main critical position is accepted, there is strictly no need for further discussion of advertising in the light of orthodox theory. It seems, however, likely to lead to a productive extension of the general critique to give further consideration to the emphasis which orthodox theory places on persuasion not only as the object of advertising but also as its chief effect.

It would appear, for one thing, that there may be a serious inconsistency in any analysis, within the accepted framework, of the effect of advertising on the long-term equilibrium of the price/output of the individual firm. Whilst agreeing that, thinking in terms of demand curves, one must see persuasion as accompanied by the outward shifting of demand curves, does this interpretation not give an important clue to the essence of the persuasive effect of advertising, in the light of the previous criticism that orthodox demand curves themselves have definitional validity only in terms of the very short period? It would appear that one might very well regard advertising, in the oligopolistic situations which I have suggested are the norm, as a weapon which might be readily adopted for reason of its immediate effects, and as one which, even though its long-term effects might be negatived by being met by countervailing expenditure by competitors, would not readily be either abandoned or reduced so long as any of those competitors continued to advertise; by the same token, the weapon would be taken up with increased vigour by some individual firm if for any reason its use happened to be (temporarily) abandoned by its competitors.

Taking the matter only thus far leaves advertising, as applied for very short-term reasons and the continued expenditure on it, as oligopolistically indeterminate, all of which fits in with the orthodox treatment. Let us pause, however, to realize that in putting the conclusion in this fashion we have indeed lost our way within the unstructured world of orthodox theory. The important point to notice is precisely that advertising itself is analysed in terms of models where all firms are in a position of analytical parity. The indeterminacy at which we paused is necessarily without any constraint from outside the firm which is being considered and as within the homogeneously-defined industry group itself.

Without going too far in detailed theorizing, suppose that we interpret such an orthodox industry group as being made up of the manufacturers of branded products. At once, this formulation forces us to realize that these are not persuading consumers to want their products in a void; they are forcing their products through to the final markets, competing both against each other and against the entrenched positions of the retailers, whether with actually-developed 'own brands' or, no less important, with the potentiality of developing such brands if manufacturers' brands' prices are high enough to make theirs competitive when sold with their own immediately available means of persuasive selling. To the extent to which a degree of rationality of the final consumer is accepted, here is a clue to the economic constraint within which apparently untrammelled advertisers work. Once again, we come back to the conclusion that we need an analysis of industrial structure, but here it must run right through from manufacturing to distribution.[1]

(This discussion also enables me to recognize the competitive importance of retailers' brands in a direct manner. Elsewhere in this book, orthodox views on retail competition, formulated only as from within the retail stage itself, have lead to the stress being on *manufacturers'* brands, with a recognition of the contribution which oligopsonist buying power may make to the cheapness of retailers' own brands being rather adduced as a factor neglected in the orthodox stress on disadvantages of price maintenance than considered positively as one which sharpens even further the potential competitiveness of retailers, as we have seen it here.)

I turn now to the further point that our discussion of advertising has also brought us up against an aspect of orthodox theory which we have not had occasion to consider in the longer-run contexts with which we have been concerned. This is its static quality. We analyse demands as though they were settled against a settled background in the world outside, any changes being introduced only for the sake of analysing one at a time the effects of changes on the new shape which our equilibrium will assume.

---

[1] In order to point my criticism of the orthodox theoretical approach to advertising, it has thus been necessary to publish here an outline of some positive theoretical lines on which I have been working. I hope to return to this at some future time but, remembering a work in which I delighted as a good 'organization' textbook years ago, I should like to note that it is a neglected feature of R. G. Hawtrey's *The Economic Problem* that he stresses the competitive importance of the interactions of manufacturers' and distributors' brands in historical industrial development.

The real world, however, is a shifting one. Dynamic changes are always occurring in the markets for many consumers' commodities. The transiency of human life itself means that today's consumers are only partly identical with yesterday's. People move into and out of the age groups which characteristically consume some commodities. Even within a stable class of commodities, taste has its swings and trade goes with them. (A manufacturer of sweet stout, for example, needs to advertise that quality if he is to take advantage of any trend towards sweetness.) For some commodities, e.g. tooth-paste for a substantial minority, individual consumers swing around quite regularly. Here, then, we may see another important function of advertising to which our textbooks pay little attention because their first principles are developed against the stable background of basic preferences and unchanged populations. Advertising may stabilize demand.

The views which have emerged in the course of my criticism seem to offer us the freedom to think again, with an awareness of the analytical importance of aspects of advertising which have not so far been brought into orthodox models. This is even more important than what I regard as the necessary abandonment of crude ideas of advertising achieving a permanent extension of a market which is based upon mere persuasion. Experience of numerous interrogations of business men by trained economists have convinced me that this mistaken view is deeply ingrained.

18. THE RELEVANCE OF THE R.P.M. CONTROVERSY

The recent British controversy over resale price maintenance provides instructive illustration of the consequences of applying the inadequately refined theoretical concepts, which I have been criticizing, to major issues of industrial practice and public policy. Seldom can a government have felt so sure of our profession's support for any drastic intervention in industrial affairs as the British Government could when it proposed to ban this restrictive practice whereby suppliers dictate the prices at which their goods may be re-sold by others. Ever since the war, with only occasional exception, publicly expressed economic opinion had condemned 'r.p.m.', and in the recent controversy the proposal to ban it was buttressed by what looked like a considerable economic case. Of those economists who contributed to public discussion, only a few opposed the ban, and hence Ministers could confidently treat them as quite unrepresentative.

As one of the exceptions, the case I tried to make was that the economic arguments which the Government repeated as conclusive were not only not conclusive against the practice but also themselves open to considerable objection. On the other hand, I thought there were economic grounds for considering that r.p.m. could be of considerable public benefit for certain kinds of product (a conclusion which had earlier been supported in the Restrictive Practices Court's judgement on the Net Book Case, where, by reason of a collective agreement, the Court had had to consider the public interest in r.p.m. as applied to books). I therefore favoured case-by-case examination if government intervention was to take place, with more open terms of reference than allowed by the eventual statute in which the Government, meeting industrial and political opposition, made some apparent relaxation of its original proposals.

The economic argument for banning r.p.m. The general argument against r.p.m. assumes that prices, and therefore retailers' gross margins, are rigidly maintained by the terms which the individual manufacturers impose on retailers. The following consequences are then thought to follow:

(1) Less efficient businesses survive more easily than they would do if retailers were free to cut prices.

(2) Because they cannot compete with other businesses directly by price reductions of the goods which are subject to r.p.m., the competition of more efficient businesses in the sale of those goods is prevented or hindered; they can compete only on the basis of 'services' outside the sale itself.

(3) Retail trade innovations often lead to reductions of costs through cutting out services; generally, r.p.m. prevents, or at least hinders, the development of new and better sorts of shops because they may not compete with price reductions on r.p.m. goods.

(4) In retail trade, services in general tend to multiply themselves even though consumers would prefer to receive cuts in prices; to allow price competition in goods at present subject to r.p.m. would at least be a blow in the right direction.

(5) It does not follow that, if r.p.m. were banned, shops which offered services would suffer. The lower prices at supermarkets, for example, would not entail that shops which cannot match those prices would have to close. They can offer services which the price-cutting shops do not give and those who want such services will pay for them. At the worst, such shops provide personal relationships with their customers and many people will gladly pay for these. The ending of r.p.m. merely means that those who would rather have the goods without such services but at lower prices will be able to exercise a choice which r.p.m. denies to them.

(6) In general, r.p.m. entails higher prices and therefore lower demands than if it were absent.[1]

[1] Mr. Nicholas Kaldor, in a letter to *The Times* (17 March 1964), contributed one argument which is not included in my list because it is not directly relevant to our present discussion of the economics of retail trade. Mr. Kaldor's point is that r.p.m. props up *manufacturers'* cartels, and he has, moreover, declared that this is where he himself sees the most serious detriment from r.p.m. He explains that, provided it is enforced, r.p.m. assures the members of a cartel (producing consumers' goods presumably) that none of them will be able to lower prices without discovery, and fear of reprisals, by others. On the other hand, he says, the proscription of r.p.m. would make it easier for manufacturers to cut prices without fear of reprisals.

As I have said, this is not directly relevant to competition in retail trade considered by itself. Looking at the matter more generally: (1) the great majority of commodities which are subject to r.p.m. are not produced by manufacturers who are members of formal cartels. Further, where there are cartels and their existence is known, they have to defend themselves before the Restrictive Practices Court and r.p.m. conditions would be a circumstance which the Court would take into account. One would therefore presume that Mr. Kaldor must be anxious about tacit

One does not need to refer these anonymous propositions to any particular model in order to criticize them. It could also be the case that many lines of reasoning converge on them and account for the conviction with which each of these propositions has seemed to be held. Further, most of the points will seem *prima facie* right, even to non-economists. It is possible that numbers (2) and (3) require some degree of sophistication of economic analysis somewhere along the line; nevertheless, all the propositions may be categorized as *prima facie* in character in so far as they confine themselves to the immediate circumstances of the problem, and do not consider how far there may be connexions between the phenomena described and other economic variables which may be relevant to the conclusions. For instance, these propositions take price and the kind of services which a consumer conceivably might choose to dispense with as the only relevant phenomena. In brief, such argument stops at the short-run introduction of the cutting of prices by businesses, restrained so far by the imposed r.p.m. conditions.

It is perhaps relevant to what follows that *prima facie* arguments on important economic matters should be considered with caution, especially when they do not need economic analysis to commend themselves to non-economists. They are precisely the kind of argument which the progressive devel-

cartels (which Mr. Kaldor is prepared to take very loosely indeed, to cover any cases where behaviour is conditioned by fear of 'price cutting', which covers short-term panic behaviour as well as longer-term low-price policies). We have already noted a propensity to favour tacit collusion as the basis for an explanation of business behaviour, influenced by the indeterminacy of orthodox monopoly theory. (2) On the other hand, Mr. Kaldor is firm on the difficulty of detecting competition in discounts, etc., allowed to retailers. In economic circumstances favouring 'price-cutting', this is not a negligible phenomenon, for it recognizedly will have a strong attraction to retailers, and increased discounts from one manufacturer might be expected to induce such sales efforts on behalf of his goods as would produce at least some of the effects of a price cut going all the way through to the stipulated r.p.m. price. So perhaps Mr. Kaldor's theoretical world is, after all, a world of tight cartels policing margins as well as prices. With reference to the real world, it should perhaps be added that agreements on margins, discounts, and other related matters have to be registered under English law and have to be defended before the Court no less than price agreements.

opment of economic thought has shown, in the past, to be incorrect when taken as the comprehensive generalizations which they appear to be. (One example is the proposition that a country which imports gold is better off than one which imports goods which it could itself produce—but that was destroyed by economic sophistication in the remote past. An example which is valid within the experience of many living economists would be the proposition that an increase of wages would diminish employment.)

Turning back to the listed propositions, one must hesitate to ascribe them to any particular economic model because of their *prima facie* character, but one could in fact refer them to a Chamberlin (large-group) type of model for a comprehensive analytical justification. One simply would have to take a model with two classes of shops, each selling the same goods, analysed in single-product terms. One class would sell the good 'with-service', the other 'without-service'. U-cost curves would, of course, be presumed to apply. The without-service class of shops should be assumed to have lower costs at a larger scale of organization than the other. In the initial circumstances, the without-service class of shops, at least, could not be in full equilibrium (except in an average-cost sense), the relationship between marginal costs and revenues having to be such that profits could be increased by lowering prices, were it not for r.p.m. Because of the r.p.m. imposed prices, the with-service shops would collectively have a larger demand than they would have under free prices, because at the imposed prices at least some customers would elect to shop where they could take the goods with the services 'for free' who would transfer their custom to the others if there were a sensible difference in price. This of course means that some of the shops which would have sold their goods without service in free conditions would in fact initially be selling them with service. . . . I do not proceed with this model because of a consideration which has been implied by this reference to it: without regard to the intellectual origin of this set of propositions, they are vulnerable to the criticisms which have been made of the kind of analysis which such a model involves, and we can therefore proceed directly to a criticism of the propositions.

The first point to be made is that the propositions are so narrowly 'single-product' in their interest. Each implicitly invites a comparison between one shop and another, as though only the prices of r.p.m. goods were involved. It is therefore possible to discuss 'efficient' versus other shops as though the incentive to the former to reduce the prices of r.p.m. goods were purely a matter of the costs and revenues associated directly with those goods. Once one admits the possibility that an r.p.m. good's price might be lowered because of additional sales from *other* goods to the customers attracted to the shop by the reductions in that price, one realizes that the price-cutting shop might even be less efficient than the others so far as the r.p.m. good is concerned. It is beside the point that it is, of course, much more difficult to decide what efficiency is, once one is out of the single-product strait jacket.

This certainly forces the issue that the shop which did not match the price cut might be unable to do so not because it had higher costs of selling and handling the r.p.m. good, but because it could not cushion itself with the profits from other goods. To take this point brings us back to what kind of 'more efficient' shop would necessarily, as the propositions assume, cut prices because in some sense its overall costs were lower than its competitors'.

The answer cannot be efficiency in the *personal* sense. It might well pay a more efficient owner-manager to take his reward in the form of extra profits at existing prices. (More efficient non-owners, like any other 'low-cost' factor of production, are unlikely to remain low-cost for long and should normally be paid more, so that the costs of the business would rise accordingly.) The only sense in which we can be sure, in the kind of abstract generalization which is involved, that greater efficiency would be associated with correspondingly lower prices, is that it must belong to a different *class* of shop so that the pressures of new-entry competition (e.g. from other retailers converting to the new form) would ensure that prices would fall to a normal level in relation to their cost. But, once we recognize classes of shops, we are back at the point that these need not be different in their efficiency, measured in any relevant way, for the one to take business away from the other by price reductions to which the latter cannot retaliate.

Of course, the actual controversy over r.p.m. recognized the force of this implicitly, when reference was made to the hard-worked example of the corner grocer's shop in the suburbs and that was contrasted with the supermarket in the shopping centre. From the wider point of view of the (over-looked) effects which a ban on r.p.m. could have on the whole trade in a particular r.p.m. commodity, we could indeed pursue that particular example. However, the errors of omission in the conclusions which we are discussing are most glaringly shown up if we revert to the distinction between specialist and general shops, made in the course of our earlier discussion.

Within these classes of shop, it is certainly easy to select examples which might very well be competing in the same shopping districts. We shall not retrace the previous argument; I shall merely illustrate it by one limited example. It stands out sufficiently that a supermarket, say, which decides to run a cut-price feature in children's books might do so only seasonally, but in any case it will select books with a very wide appeal. Equally it is hard to be precise about the sense in which it might be said to be more 'efficient' at this, except that it sells a lot, and that does not settle any of the cost questions which efficiency involves and which single-product analysis seems to show as easy to settle. It might, we can see, pay the supermarket to sell a lot, even if it lost on each actual transaction, on the average, so far as concerns the costs which can be added up in relation to the cut-price books, provided that it made up for this because the customers for the books went out with sufficient quantities of other goods.

At the same time, for the book trade to be damaged, it would not be necessary for the cut-price books to be of the kind which the specialist bookshop would ordinarily feature prominently in its regular stocks; they could equally be classics whose cheap sales will attract to the supermarket customers ordinarily dealing elsewhere who might buy some of the higher-profit special foodstuffs as well as taking care of more humdrum requirements while they are there. In any case the bookshop, being also a multi-product shop, will lose in a similarly adventitious manner not only the sale of the books concerned but also other books that it might have sold at the same time.

The competitiveness of the bookshop will certainly not be hampered by high costs or low efficiency in the sale of, e.g., children's books, and we need not argue that the mother, out on a general shopping expedition, will think of the pleasant chat she might have had in the bookshop and decide to pay 2d. extra for that. What hampers the bookshop are the costs of being a bookshop, and although the princes of the trade may provide substantial credit, the costs of being a bookshop even in the case of these are dominated by the costs of the general stocks on which it must build its trade, and the costs of the single copy orders which it must be prepared to get if its kind of trade is to continue.[1] If it matches the price cut or puts the cut-price books out of its display, it will have to make up its loss from the sales of other books, and it certainly has not the basis to hit back whilst still remaining recognizably a bookshop.

The 'service' which consumers lose if such shops decrease sharply in number is not something that they could 'pay for' deliberately when they weigh the choice of the cut-price and the standard price purchase. It is indeed a before-sales service which they may use, so long as it exists, to select and approve the very books which the supermarket offers before they purchase from the latter. This brings out the point that popular economic argument may induce serious errors of thinking when it classifies customers into persons who choose to buy

---

[1] The Judgment in the English Restrictive Practices Court case on the Net Book Agreement rejected assertions that this was a service which the consumer might be made to pay for separately: 'We accept that as a matter of business common sense it is not practicable for booksellers to charge for any of these services; the cost of them must be regarded as part of the bookseller's overhead expenses.' (*Judgment*, taken from the *Transcript*, p. 17.)

without service and those who enjoy the goods sold with service, separately. The mother who buys the cut-price children's books may none the less greatly appreciate the bookshop as the source of her own books. In being led to take the one trade away, she may well have helped deprive herself of the facilities she enjoys in the other, and there will be small inducement even for the enterprising supermarket to take on any extensive general book department. Browsing customers could play havoc with the massive throughput of goods on which its organization depends.

The services which multiply themselves with increasing wealth and spending power are not only credit and delivery services, which might indeed be specially charged for; they include the services of speciality shops with wider ranges of stocks of kinds which previously had to be got to special order and could not then attract customers by being there to be seen and taken away. At least some of the modern 'better sorts' of shops will be of this kind, and their survival could be affected by the price freedom which would enable the supermarket to increase its hold on the grocery and household goods trade, even if their sales overlapped only to a relatively small extent in the initial conditions after a ban on r.p.m.

Of course, some speciality shops will survive; but the interim period of price-cutting damage could have other permanent effects besides a decrease in the number of specialists. Manufacturers of minor brands of goods will have lost the basis on which at present they build up their trade. The shelves of the supermarkets will be for their own brands and for the leading national brands only. To go into the competitive significance of this would indeed take us back into earlier discussions. But in a society whose avowed aim is to be more competitive, it deserves mention that the efficiency of the large manufacturers is partly kept in condition by the competition from smaller makers trying to displace them.

In one way or another, the present line of thought has damaged the simple one-way deductions of four of the anti-r.p.m. propositions, without our having exhausted the argument which could be derived from the theoretical discussion earlier in this book. Two which still require frontal attack are the first and the sixth propositions.

The first proposition, linking the survival of inefficient shops with the price of particular goods, involves, of course, the fallacy of the marginal business. Thinking in single-product terms and accepting that a business *must* cover its costs if it is to survive, it is easy to argue as if the price of an r.p.m. good must cover the costs of the supplier who is just hanging on in that trade. Without doing more than refer to the indeterminacy of individual costs which the proposition brushes aside, we may pause on the major point that marginal businesses in retail trade notoriously do not survive. Marginal businesses, however, are always with us because their vacant shops are taken over by others. This turnover of shops at the margin means that we get the services of marginal shops without their turnover 'covering' their long-run costs. Some element in the supply of many commodities always comes on these terms. If the rate of bankruptcy of the 'corner shop' were to increase somewhat it does not even follow that there would be fewer corner shops. It would simply mean that vacant corner shops were more frequently available for those who wished to try their luck, admittedly with their chances injured by the narrowing of the trade for their class of shops. Once again, the case may be different with the shopping district speciality shop which will have to pay the rent needed to keep its premises from being absorbed by a turnover-hungry supermarket; and in the initial period of excess competition in this 'new' kind of shop, rents may rise above their long-term value sufficiently to remove permanently specialists who might otherwise have survived. The subsequent vacancies will be large premises needing costly conversion back to suit the specialist.

Proposition (6) which we turn to finally deserves to be ranked as the *pons asinorum* (the Euclid i. 5) of economics. It requires a very large part of a teacher's skill to get his pupils to see all the considerations, *ceteris paribus*, which must be taken into account before they can confidently argue with the help of *the* demand curve that a reduction in price will mean an increase in demand for a commodity, and go on to consider what factors will make the increase of demand greater or smaller for a given fall of price. When students leave the classroom, however, all too often the subtleties fall away, the diagrams remain.

Among the considerations which are too lightly passed over even in formal exposition, in the analysis which at this elementary level is concerned with isolated markets, are those affecting the distribution stage at which consumer goods are ordinarily sold. Too much has to be learned about the costs of production which dominate the cost functions which are then discussed. But 'stocks' do not ordinarily loom large in the basic teaching of economists, just because the great truths in the principles of elementary economics of value are most easily expounded in a context of consumers with given tastes and knowing what commodities they will buy at given prices.

That some wants are, at any one time, not committed to particular goods and still less to particular brands of goods, however, besides being an obvious thing once it is stated, is also a truth of detail which is relevant to problems with which economists have to grapple in our time. That kind of truth is not carried forward by demand curves which ignore the rôle of stocks and of the shops which offer them. A number of reasons have already been given for the conclusion that stocks may be a factor in the generation of the demand curve itself, and very simple economic analysis would establish the proposition that the short-term determinateness of the selling prices of r.p.m. goods may be a factor which encourages their being stocked. There are other factors which could be mentioned, such as the importance for the total demand of some commodities that shops and stocks should be widely dispersed if total demand is to be maintained. But, if one wishes to catch a horse, a lasso around one hoof should be enough.

Our brief glance at retail distribution in the light of the r.p.m. controversy and the *prima facie* economic propositions which have been applied in it, will at least have shown that here also there is room for more refinement of analysis. It will also have reinforced the broad conclusion to which this book has been tending—that a dominant system of economic theory on which economists are currently trained needs critical modification. The very form in which its generalizations are developed, as we have seen, may prevent apposite analysis of the distributive sectors of the economy. But we meet these difficulties especially sharply here just because the theory is actually *being applied to an individual industry*, for we have already seen that the system of analysis which we have been criticizing *prevents* the proper consideration of industries as subject-matter.

*   *   *   *

GENERAL CONCLUSION

The concept of an industry is surely the gateway to a theoretical study of an industrial economy. The theory of the firm needs to be extended to become a theory of industrial economics before we can take up in this micro area the questions which we handle so confidently in the macro area. Much indeed of our speculation in the macro area (e.g. concerning aggregate investment) involves the search for propositions which need to have validity in the narrower sectors of the economy where policies impinge. The problem of 'disaggregation' cannot be handled in the abstract with any pretension to reliability on the basis of currently accepted theory, for there is no analytical bridge from the economy as a whole to the individual firm which is the ultimate agent and subject of policy. A theory which has to leave out the industry as a subject of analytical interest is a more tenuous guide to knowledge than current enthusiasms for policy recommendations would suggest.

INDEX

PRINTED IN GREAT BRITAIN
BY R. & R. CLARK, LTD., EDINBURGH